I0438397

Navigating These Challenging Times

Navigating These Challenging Times

What to Expect and How to Travel the Road

Josiane d'Hoop

iUniverse, Inc.
Bloomington

Navigating These Challenging Times
What to Expect and How to Travel the Road

Copyright © 2010, 2011 by Josiane d'Hoop.

All rights reserved. No part of this book may be used or reproduced by any means, graphic, electronic, or mechanical, including photocopying, recording, taping or by any information storage retrieval system without the written permission of the publisher except in the case of brief quotations embodied in critical articles and reviews.

iUniverse books may be ordered through booksellers or by contacting:

iUniverse
1663 Liberty Drive
Bloomington, IN 47403
www.iuniverse.com
1-800-Authors (1-800-288-4677)

Because of the dynamic nature of the Internet, any web addresses or links contained in this book may have changed since publication and may no longer be valid. The views expressed in this work are solely those of the author and do not necessarily reflect the views of the publisher, and the publisher hereby disclaims any responsibility for them.

Any people depicted in stock imagery provided by Thinkstock are models, and such images are being used for illustrative purposes only.
Certain stock imagery © Thinkstock.

ISBN: 978-1-4620-2543-5 (pbk)
ISBN: 978-1-4620-2542-8 (clth)
ISBN: 978-1-4620-2541-1 (ebk)

Library of Congress Control Number: 2011909018

Printed in the United States of America

iUniverse rev. date: 06/27/2011

CONTENTS

Introduction

I have been a student and a teacher of metaphysics for twenty years. I have primarily studied the teachings of Alice Bailey and Djwhal Khul, whose groundbreaking collaboration during the first half of the twentieth century brought powerful additions to the teaching of the Ageless Wisdom to humanity. Through this teaching, and as a result of my own work and its application with many clients, I have developed a relatively deep understanding of metaphysics, which forms the basis of the information presented in this book. I have, however, tried to adapt those complex teachings to our present situation and the difficult times in which we live. The Master of the Ageless Wisdom, Djwhal Khul, has given us, through influential writer and theosophist Alice A. Bailey, much information to draw upon to understand the role and responsibility of humanity in this development, as well as the ineluctable energy movement to which we are submitted. It is far beyond our power to stop the transformation process already underway.

Understanding the world we live in and the transformation awaiting us can give us both power and wisdom: the power to be a participant in this evolution and the wisdom to let go of our fears and conflicted personal expectations. We can experience fear and destruction, being tossed by the energy as if we were caught in a hurricane, or we can be in the eye of the hurricane, remaining centered within ourselves and experiencing peace. My hope for this book is to offer an understanding of what we are going through, as well as some practical tools we can all use to reach and keep our centeredness.

Chapter 1 -
The Year 2012

The year 2012 often generates an array of emotions, from fear to hope to simple curiosity. It marks the end of the Mayan calendar, and in view of the occurring Earth changes, people have started wondering whether there is anything about this date to be concerned with.

Many people have heard that 2012 is going to bring the end of the world—Armageddon, or the Rapture, as described in Scriptures—when in fact 2012 will mark the change from one age to another. This does not imply that there is nothing we need to prepare ourselves for, as change always brings challenges. The Rapture described in the Scriptures is not intended to represent the destruction of humanity for the purpose of its enlightenment. The Rapture represents the rising into the light of our darkest thoughts and our hateful emotions—the non-evolved consciousness in ourselves—in order to transmute them into love and compassion.

Let's look at the year 2012 from different angles:

Numerology: 2012 represents a shift in consciousness for all in order to accommodate a new paradigm. In terms of numerology,

2012 reduces to the number five (add all the numbers in 2012 together). From a numerological point of view, it is a year of change and transformation. It carries the resonance that will allow higher consciousness to impact the mind of humanity. Yet evolution happens through a succession of crises. A crisis is the rise of energy that accumulates until it explodes, dissolves, and gives place to new vibrations and perceptions. We have entered such a period, and we will experience these crises over the next two decades.

Astrology: From an astrological point of view, 2012 represents a cosmic crisis for the earth itself and therefore for all living entities upon it. The transformation in the "etheric," or energetic, body of the earth during this period will be induced by the infiltration of energy from Sirius and from the constellation of the Great Bear. This new vibration will be received and anchored in the etheric body of the earth, transforming the consciousness of all lives within it, including the consciousness of humanity. We absorb this cosmic energy through our meridians and distribute it through our chakra system, or energetic centers, located in our own etheric bodies. Our energetic constitution is a small replica of the constitution of the planet in the same way that an atom has the same energetic constitution as a human. Like in the human body, the earth has its own grid of subtle energy channels. Some of them are called "lei lines." They are conduits for the flow of energy through the earth's body.

Our chakra system is composed principally of seven major centers: the first is the root chakra at the base of the spine; the second is the sacral center at the height of the belly button; the third is the solar plexus in the area of the diaphragm; the fourth is the heart center between the shoulder blades; the fifth is the throat center at the throat level; the sixth is the "ajna" center (the "third eye") just above the eyebrows in the middle of the forehead; and the seventh is the crown chakra on the top of the head. These centers have different functions and receive energy from different vibrational levels.

The root center at the base of the spine is the corresponding chakra to the etheric body. Our etheric body is the level of energy closest to the physical body. It contains the replica of our physical organs and of our nervous system; these "etheric nerves" are called "nadis." Through our etheric body, the pranic energy, the energy that feeds and allows our body to sustain life, is received and circulates, bringing life and vitality to our physical body. The next level is our emotional body, which stores and creates our emotions; its corresponding chakra is the sacral center. The third energetic level is our mental body or concrete mind, containing and producing our thoughts. Its corresponding chakra is the solar plexus.

Within the body of the earth, the root chakra is represented by the mineral kingdom, its sacral center by the vegetable kingdom, its solar plexus center by the animal kingdom, and its heart center by humanity.

The earth, like any other living entity, continues to evolve. This new cosmic energy from Sirius and the Great Bear is coming to help the earth in this evolution. The immediate progression of the earth is to open its heart chakra and to restructure this center in order to accommodate the new heightened planetary vibration; therefore, we, humanity, being the heart center of the earth, will be pushed to transform as well. Transformation and destruction are inevitable, as all creation requires the destruction of the old structures for the construction of the new ones. These structures may be corporations, financial institutions, or old ways of living, but also at times physical lives. Now more than ever we need to remember that even when lives are lost (such as in an earthquake), physical bodies are only the envelope of the life within. The soul—the higher consciousness of all forms—is really who we are and remains intact, elevated, and renewed.

In his book *On Reincarnation*, America's greatest psychic, Edgar Cayce, describes life, death, and reincarnation in a very colorful way. To paraphrase, he asks us to imagine ourselves as souls before we return to Earth, being on a ship in the Caribbean on a beautiful sunny day. Through the clear water we see the wreck of a boat that had been transporting a treasure. We decide to go and explore, so we put on a diving suit with lead boots and a heavy helmet that obstructs our vision. We jump overboard and reach the ocean floor, thinking that this expedition will be easy, that we just have to go to the wreck and retrieve the treasure. Yet we have not taken into account the force of the currents, the cumbersome suit we are wearing (our physical body), and the occasional disappearance of the light when a cloud obstructs the sun. As we fight our way to the wreck, our body becomes weary, and we become confused by the difficulty of the task. We feel threatened by the appearance of several sharks circling, and our air hose has become tangled in the beams of the wreck. We start wondering what we are doing here. The peaceful place on the boat and the beautiful ocean become unreal. All we see is the battle we have to fight here, keeping our eyes on the sharks as they move closer. We lose sight of our original goal. Yet as we become more and more wary and exhausted, we are hauled back up onto the deck of the boat again, rescued, and freed from our heavy suit.

In these times of change, it is important for every one of us to realize that we are not limited to our physical body; our soul uses a body and a personality to express itself, and every incarnation allows the soul, our real self, to evolve through our experiences and difficulties while in physical life. We are the soul, and therefore we benefit from this advancement in every succeeding incarnation.

The personality always resists change because of the fear of the unknown and the lack of understanding of the higher purpose for change. Yet the soul can give us direction, information, and understanding, and in these challenging times, it can be of great importance to keep this connection open. In spite of the weariness we might experience, this level of ourselves, our soul, is our guiding star.

The intensity of destruction we will witness as we get closer to 2012 will be directly related to the level of evolution of every one of us individually and of humanity as a whole. The larger the number of people intending to connect with their soul, bringing in higher frequencies of light, the easier and more harmonious the transition will be. Resistance creates pain and chaos. Therefore, we need to focus on the benefit of this transformative time rather than fear it, thus allowing the energy to flow unimpeded. This new energy will then be integrated and anchored in our personality and in the body of the earth, bringing much progress and relief.

Because most of us do not have the ability to perceive the higher purpose of world events, we judge them solely from a physical perspective. When natural disasters occur, taking thousand of lives, it creates a mass reaction of compassion and solidarity, thereby opening our hearts. This is the higher purpose of such events. The people involved who sacrifice their lives for others will gain good karma for their next incarnation or will get rid of a bad karma they were burdened with. In any case, they will gain because of the sacrifice they made helping humanity open up to love. Of course this decision is not made from the personality level; it is made by the soul in agreement with the personality and is rarely consciously known by the individual.

We live in the earth's energy, and so do the vegetable and animal kingdoms. We are responsible for the transfer of consciousness to them, as they are in levels of evolution below us. Higher levels of consciousness are always responsible for helping or hindering the lives and consciousnesses of those below them. Energy travels down; the higher consciousnesses can access the lower, but the lowest, limited by "the ring pass not," or energetic barrier are not able to access the highest until they have evolved enough to reach and sustain the vibrations of the next more evolved level. This energetic barrier is naturally created by the different vibrational rates found on each level. We can only access the next level by raising our vibrations.

The "devic" or angelic kingdom rules the elements of the earth. The angelic kingdom evolves parallel to the human kingdom; we are interdependent and are helping one another in our progression. In the angelic kingdom, the lower levels of consciousness are composed of devas of different degrees of evolution, who, as they evolve, will become the "white angels," the equivalent of the Masters of the Wisdom in the human hierarchy. Being part of our energy field, the devas will also be touched by this incoming energy. If humanity welcomes this higher, more-evolved energy instead of fearing it, it will help the devic Kingdom rise along with us to new levels. This evolution will result in a positive effect on the quality of the air, the water, the weather patterns, and of the earth itself. Our impact on the environment is directly related to the quality of our thoughts and emotions. We influence the environment not only through our actions; we affect the devas of nature by the energy we transfer to them through our energy field. Therefore, the less we fear this transition, the less negatively we affect them. Consequently, the less we fear this transition, the less the Devic Kingdom will be negatively impacted. The dissolution of our fears will allow us to witness positive changes in the environment.

When humanity produces thoughts of love and harmony, these thoughts touch every consciousness, every atom constituting every form of life on Earth—plants, water, the body of Earth itself. Cosmic law teaches us that higher vibrations dissolve lower vibrations. When the highly evolved energy of Sirius and the Great Bear penetrate the etheric body of the earth, along with the new constellation of Aquarius, transformation will occur.

The challenge for humanity is to look at the transformation as a benefit for the elevation of the human mind, transcending the fears it may generate.

As time passes, we will experience more disturbances in the world, such as the reorganization of our financial institutions or the difficult weather patterns. The activation of the energy that needs to be transformed will inevitably cause chaos. The necessity to dissolve those energies will force us to raise our consciousness in order to resolve the issues that have been created by the less-evolved, unaware people. Humanity will be called to make choices: we can choose to continue responding to the divisive, fearful ways of our personality or we can decide to follow the call of our heart, to exercise compassion and understanding. If we react to the fear generated by aggression with violence, no matter where it comes from, we are contributing to the rise of violence. Violence will always engender violence; it cannot produce peace. Keep in mind that through the law of karma, whatever we send out comes back to us.

The application of the law "higher vibration dissolves lower vibration" can be used to dissolve lower thought forms and bring higher truth to the mind of human kind. Aggression cannot be resolved by war. Fear engenders more fear, when, in turn, understanding and compassion will dissolve them. By rising to the wisdom of the soul and being in our heart, we can dissolve the energy generated by lower emotions, thus fostering good relationships, including the mutual acceptance of our differences. Everyone carries negative and positive energy: negative being less evolved and related to the personality, positive being more evolved and related to the higher consciousness. This means that everyone is capable of the most despicable intention, as well as the most honorable one, given the appropriate circumstances for each individual. The maturity of the soul is the determinant factor to differentiate which of us are more or less likely to express the positive aspect of his or her being.

Some are still in the infancy stage while others are completing their cycle of incarnations. While some are teachers and some are students, we need to remember that we are all students in need of instruction or wisdom on some level as long as we are in human form. Being human means we are imperfect; therefore, we all have something to learn. No one should feel superior or think he or she is in possession of a greater truth than someone else. This humility will eventually make each of us realize we are one with humanity: that the individuals we dislike are in fact sharing the same soul, experiencing the same difficulties, striving for the same desire for happiness and love. The personality encourages our notion of separation because of the mind's perception and comparison of differences. Just as we would not reject flowers of different colors and shapes, we should not reject people who are different from us. In fact, we can come to recognize the individuals who cause us the most pain and discomfort as opportunities to grow grace, just as a grain of sand in an oyster begins as an irritation but turns into a beautiful pearl.

The fear of lack engenders greed, jealousy, and competitiveness, along with other negative values. We think we need to take from others because there might not be enough resources for everyone. We horde possessions to gain security and power, when in fact there is no real security or power without the involvement of our soul and the protection from our Higher Self—a part of our divine self we also call our guardian angel. This angelic being guides us in the development of our personality and eventually brings us to the connection with our soul. Our Higher Self brings circumstances to us throughout our lives that present us with opportunities for growth in maturity and in consciousness. Our Higher Self watches over us, guides and protects us, and helps us with particulars when we ask.

We live in the illusion of separation and try to control our lives in order to feel safe. We fail to realize that in any particular

8

life, we will go through the experiences that our soul needs for its own growth and development. Even though our personality might decide its own course of action, it will not be without pain and difficulties if those choices are too far away from the soul's path. Unhappiness comes from resistance and the inability to express the soul's intention. When we are in the flow of creation, we experience synchronized opportunities, success, and joy. Soul qualities are expressed when understanding and acceptance of others' differences is predominant in one's mind. When judgment and criticism rule, we are tapping into the lower, non-evolved part of our personality. Such separative feelings do not exist at the level of the soul.

The coming of 2012 and the raising of the lower energies being generated is forcing us to evolve. Pain will be experienced as a means of progress, as unfortunately, humanity evolves through pain. Pain is our motivator for change, as often we would gladly stay where we are if we were happy there. Pain motivates us to do something different to stop such difficult feelings. While the experience of pain is a catalyst for human evolution, it is, however, only temporary, and its duration is determined by us. Once we understand the reason or the higher purpose of a situation, we stop resisting, we get the lesson it brings, and we move out of the pain. Pain is only created by the resistance to change and our inability to move forward, or to grasp the lesson. When one perceives the value and higher purpose of any painful circumstance, pain disappears and consciousness rises. For example, if we all could understand and hold in our consciousness the knowledge that any difficulty we experience during challenging times is there for the greatest good of humanity, the changes and challenges would not be as difficult to accept.

Individually, we all experience situations of a similar nature in which the resistance to change results in needless suffering. After not getting a job that she very much wanted, one of my clients became distraught. And yet, a couple of months later, she was led to change her career altogether and is very happy to be on a new path. She feels blessed every day, probably because she is in alignment with her soul's direction.

We all have great inner resources to rise to the challenges of any conflict when we believe in our higher purpose. We see this when men and women sacrifice their lives in times of war. The threshold of 2012 is here to eradicate wars and yet will require courage and dedication. Situations will be created to teach humanity that wars only engender more violence, and that only right human relationships through love and understanding will bring peace and unity. We, humanity, through our response to those situations are directly responsible for the level of pain that will be necessary for our evolution. The faster we open our minds, the more harmonious the transition will be.

As we apply this principle to our own lives, we should try to accept and be tolerant of those with whom we disagree. Realize that from where they stand, their beliefs are what they see. Your truth might be different, but it is only because you are seeing things from a different angle. This does not make them or you wrong. Everyone changes places and vibrations at any given time, and this always brings new perception. As teenagers, we are so sure of what we believe, often only to realize as we get older how little we knew. This is the experience of humanity as a whole. The more we progress, the more we realize how little we know. We become more and more accepting of others. For some it is experienced in one lifetime, for others it will take several lifetimes to come to this conclusion. Whatever our individual journey, we need to help one another so we can all be lifted above the difficult conditions we might encounter either physically or emotionally. As humanity reaches soul consciousness, the light of the soul will come down and illuminate the lower, non-evolved part of our nature. We are all involved in this transformation and in this elevation of consciousness, and that is what 2012 is about.

Books and articles will be distributed all over the world, convincing many that the end is at hand. This is not the truth. Humanity does not work alone, and the destiny of life on Earth is not solely up to us. A lot of work is done and attention given from the other side of the veil or the astral plane. The consciousness of too many life forms would be affected by the downfall of humanity.

If it is true that purification is necessary, it is monitored and helped from higher levels of consciousness and other more evolved beings—not only because they want to help humanity, but because too much is at stake for them as well, through the interconnectedness of energy linking us all. The body of the earth affects the other planets in the solar system as much as they, in turn, affect Earth. The notion of separation is an illusion. This includes the misperception of separation amongst the various races and countries making up humanity, amidst the unseen sharing of our energy with that of the animals and vegetation surrounding us, as well as within the relationships between the earth, the sun, and the other planets.

We will not be permitted to destroy the earth, because it would affect the creation and evolution of our whole solar system. Corrective divine intervention is always possible and might be necessary to save the earth if humanity does not align to divine purpose. If this were to happen, the earth would survive, but humanity would be delayed in its development for hundreds of thousands of years. This is not part of the divine plan, so help is given from many sources to prevent destruction from happening.

The assistance given comes primarily from the Pleiades, who represent the higher consciousness, or soul of the earth. Those planets have the same great influence on the earth that our soul has on us individually. The Pleiadiens are helped in their mission to stabilize the earth by the Anteriens, beings coming from the star Antaris. Their intervention is such that it appeases the energy set in motion by human emotions, thus preventing too great a reaction among the devas and elementals forming the astral plane, as well as the four elements on Earth (earth, air, fire, and water). Beyond these elements, the Pleiadiens and Anteriens also bring balance to the vegetable kingdom and to all that is directly related to the life on Earth and to the ecosystem. The damage already done by humanity because of our selfishness and ignorance has caused the earth to be out of balance; consequently, the lives in every kingdom of nature have been affected. This effect could be even more dramatic if changes are not forthcoming and implemented in a speedy way. Help can be and is given in order for us to take the necessary steps to correct our mistakes and realize fully how we affect the whole. Indications of the impact of humanity on the earth include dramatic weather patterns, climatic changes, and destructive fires. These so-called natural phenomena are mostly responses to the thoughts we project and hold in our mind and to our emotional activity. If we do not drastically change our behaviors, thought processes, and angry emotions, we will face greater challenges until we truly understand the effect we have on our environment.

The help given by those higher beings, the Pleiadiens and the Anteriens, is vibrational in nature. This help can prevent devastating earthquakes, volcanic eruptions, and even weather patterns that would destroy crops on a large scale, endangering the very survival of animals and humans. Not everything can be averted though, as we have to face the effects of our actions. Help is given because humanity in its infancy does not have the full consciousness of its actions. So we can be assured that we are not alone, and that beings far beyond our average capacity to perceive and understand are aiding us in our evolution. Just as humanity is receiving this assistance as a whole, our soul and Higher Self are aiding us individually, at the personal level. As we grow, we will first identify and then learn to moderate our thoughts and feelings; then together we will be able to consciously participate in the evolution of the earth.

Chapter 2 -
Path to Transformation

When we entered this new millennium, we came under the energetic vibration of the number two. This number calls for unity: unity with our environment, with other countries, with nature, unity with everyone we interact with. Ultimately, it calls for unity with our soul. This is the achievement that will take place during this millennium. We have left behind the vibration of the number one, which is related to individuality, in order for us to discover and experience relationships under the number two vibration.

How do we go from here to there, moving forward toward unity? The answer: through altruism. Each and every time someone does something kind for someone else without any intentional expectation of personal gain in return, humanity progresses. Every time an individual participates in bringing the light of the divine into this lower realm of consciousness, everyone benefits. Every time someone refrains from anger or hatred, from gossip or jealousy, he or she is disempowering darkness and freeing himself or herself from its hold.

The echo of the ancient times is revealing the hidden darkness that needs to be brought out to the light to be transformed. It exposes past memories often buried deep in our subconscious. Our conscious mind is only 10 percent of our mental body, while the subconscious mind occupies up to 90 percent. This unexamined and unresolved past is like a cancer that tags humanity with lower thought forms and emotions that handicap its ability to express beauty. Individually, there are several ways we can try to heal the pain from our past. We can suppress it, try to ignore it, scab over it, hoping that time will eventually take care of it. This is what we most often do, when we do not know what to do about pain. More effectively, we can also confront the pain of our past by going within, and through self-exploration, bring to consciousness the root of the pain. This will offer us the greatest opportunity to completely heal the very things that have poisoned us incarnation after incarnation, or year after year. Because our subconscious mind is patterned through feelings, not through thoughts, exploration methods like hypnotherapy and regression therapy can greatly help. We can also choose on some level to remove ourselves from life in physical form and escape dealing with it, at least for now; or, finally, we can surrender, face our demons, feel the pain, and release it all to our soul for healing.

The first method of dealing with pain, "Letting time take care of it," is the path of least resistance that humanity has more or less followed until now. This is no longer an effective choice, as we are now called to heal our pain in order to evolve and thus become able to sustain the new coming vibrations. Evolution requires that darkness be brought to the light to be transformed and raised to a higher vibration. When one does not take care of his own healing and of its rhythm, the pressure forced upon him through life experiences presented by his Higher Self can be quite difficult to sustain. It is an unavoidable process though, as this brings the progression necessary to allow the soul to connect with the physical self and use the personality as its tool for divine expression on the physical plane, as it has always been intended by design. Because our Higher Self pushes us to evolve, lessons in life become more painful until they are learned. If we choose to ignore the first signal, those signals will continue to come and will become louder until we cannot ignore them anymore. If we misuse the energy of money, for example, wasting it with no consciousness of its value, we will experience times of lack along our life. This is designed to gradually lead us to a greater respect for this energy, using it with gratitude instead of carelessness.

The second option, "To go in and heal from the inside out," is what a larger number of us are starting to do. This path appeals to a more elevated soul and developed consciousness. Even though it is sometimes difficult work, the reward is certainly comparable to the size of the effort. Life's flavor is much sweeter when we do this, following the Scriptures' direction of "heal thyself first." The growth in psychotherapy and related fields and the boom in self-help literature attest to the fact that more and more, people are choosing to take their growth in hand, heal their pain, and learn their lessons—whether they realize they are being guided by the Higher Self is irrelevant; the lessons are being learned.

A number of us at this time will choose the third option, even if it is only subconsciously, "To remove themselves from life in physical form", because they are incapable of sustaining the new vibrations or unwilling to face the difficulty and the emotional strain of the turmoil. They will do this through the many modes of releasing life from the body: illness, accident, war, or Earth changes. This last option will periodically become a choice for humanity. We have already seen mass exodus in the form of the tsunami in Indonesia or the earthquake in Haiti. Painful as it is to witness from the personality perspective, we must take heart in the knowledge that life never ends—it just changes form, and those who depart do so with the full guidance and cooperation of their soul, which is who they truly are. Their work continues on the other side, and the separation is, after all, a temporary illusion. I have had experiences in my life where I have helped people transition out of their body; they have given me great confidence in this process.

I would like to share one of those experiences to help you to gain insight and confidence in the afterlife. A friend of mine, an elderly man, had lung cancer and was in the hospital with pneumonia. He was so afraid of dying that he asked the doctors to keep him on life support no matter what. When I went to see him in the hospital, I received spiritual guidance that he would die in nine days. When he saw me, he immediately asked me about his prognosis. I told him that he would be okay, as I knew he would be, once he reached the other side. On the eighth day, his wife called me, saying he was on oxygen support and that the doctor was now referring to her to make a decision about how to proceed. Her husband was unconscious, only breathing through the ventilation machine. I told her to wait until the next morning—as guidance said nine days, there was no need to rush to take him off of the machine.

On the morning of the ninth day, as I prepared for my daily meditation, he surprised me by visiting me on the astral plane. He was angry at me and told me I had lied to him by telling him he would be okay. Of course I defended myself, reminding him that he was too afraid of dying for me to relay to him what guidance had communicated to me, and that what I told him was, in fact, what I knew to be true—that he would truly be fine once on the other side. Hearing that he would be fine, he was then able to relax, let go, and gently pass over without resistance. After we chatted for a bit, he asked me to call his wife and to tell her to have him taken off life support. He was not afraid anymore and was eager to leave his body behind.

I called his wife right away. She was not there, so I left a message on her answering machine. I went on with my day, and around 2:00 PM that afternoon, I brought myself back to a meditative state, as I had some remote healings to perform. My friend was back again, making contact with me from the other side. He was very impatient and anxious, telling me that the tubes had not been removed from his nose yet and insisted that I call his wife once more. I reached his wife, who had just come home and had been listening to her messages. After talking with me, she called the hospital and instructed the doctor to take her husband off life support. An hour later, his body was dead. This man's consciousness stayed around for a couple of days, very interested in the distant healings I was performing, and in observing the projection and movement of energy. Then he said goodbye to me and left for another plane. Although I am still able to talk to him when I call on him, his soul has moved to another level.

If we choose not to do the necessary healing work or do not recognize the need to do it, we go through life experiencing painful lessons. As the lessons become too difficult to bear, we eventually call on God for help; our Higher Self answers the call, and progress is finally made. So we have options, and we are called to choose how we want to enter this transformative phase of development. There is no free will for deciding where we are going, but there are choices as to how we get there.

The development of consciousness is felt way beyond what humanity perceives. This development is not just about us. It is also about other energy substances, other consciousnesses, like the elements of the earth, the water, and the air. It is about the evolution of the trees, the plants, and all the related eco-systems. It is about the evolution of God himself, the one in whom we live and move and have our being. Humanity is a major transformation center for those other less-evolved consciousnesses, because we are the most evolved beings in physical form upon the earth. We are the beings who have a mind and a distinct consciousness. We have evolved as individual souls, whereas other life forms share a group soul. At this time we are called to speed up the development and to heal and transform what we have created in previous incarnations when we were not as conscious or as aware. Nobody can do this for us. This is the law of karma. We have to reap what we have sown. The beauty of a time like this is that we will have the possibility to start anew, transformed and supported by higher consciousness. It will allow us to really see the present as the "Dark Age," where most people have been living in fear and pain on our planet. Are we going to let the forces of our lower personality drag us down into despair, anger, and pain, or will we choose to bring in the light to dissipate the darkness? Will we shy away from our responsibilities, or will we rise to the tremendous opportunities we are presented with and use our empowered strength and creativity to move through our limitations and the status quo?

This world belongs to us. If we are incarnated at this time, it is because we have chosen to be here. With great difficulties also come great opportunities. We have come here to participate in this transformation and to free ourselves from old karmas and energies that have held us down for ages. This is our time to bring newness of thoughts and actions to all institutions that need reform. There will be new ways for leaders in all areas of society to transform the corrupt, inefficient, and outdated ways and lead humanity with more integrity, sincerity, unity, and compassion.

For some, this vision is considered Utopia—an impossibility. The idea that this change can't happen and that things will always be the same is the inherited belief tenaciously holding us back. And this is why transformation will happen through dramatic events, if we do not choose to participate in the change right now, using our own free will. Change will then be forced upon us in order to move humanity from our orientation of selfishness to one guided by our heart.

Pain has always been the tool that forces us to progress, as we only seem to change things in our lives in order to avoid pain. It took WWII for us to create the United Nations and to generate the desire of the European nations to be united in spite of thousand of years of war between Germany, France, England, and others.

Each of us will one day awaken to the truth that is relevant for us, whether it be regarding war, or money, or relationships. The challenging times we are living in are here to help us in this awakening. This time of transformation is not to be feared but should be welcomed and regarded as the beginning of a new era. Truth will allow us to step into a new level of consciousness where we will participate in the creation of our lives with deliberate intent, under the guidance of our soul helping us to dissipate our fears, and to establish new ways of interaction with each other and our community.

Keep in mind that energy follows thoughts. Through the law of attraction, we empower what we focus upon. Every action has a reaction. Turn your attention to the soul, and you will be in the flow of the universe. Resist the soul's intent and you will experience struggle. It is a simple, observable fact. Most of us have been in one or more situations where we wanted something so badly that we dismissed our inner voice of guidance and proceeded toward our goal with determination, ignoring all the signs put on our path to stop us. Often it resulted in hardship, and we realized we had made a mistake. We could have avoided it had we not been blinded by our desires. Yet at other times, we may have felt everything was easy; opportunities came our way as if everything was open to us. This is being in the flow of the source.

We can experience more of those moments when we align with our soul. However, many of us do not know how to bring ourselves in alignment with our soul. Know that every time we express love, we are in this alignment. Every time we choose a positive thought over a negative one, we come closer to the expression of the soul. Every time we render service or demonstrate kindness, we rise closer to the soul. It takes re-patterning of the normal tendencies of the personality, instinctually oriented toward selfishness, to achieve soul connection. This work takes awareness and willingness but also brings much happiness and great freedom from the fears and the venomous projection of negative thoughts that invariably come back to us through the law of karma. Progress can be measured by small steps.

I had a client who was so angry, he made his own life and those around him miserable. Yet, through the hard work of self-discovery and self-discipline over a period of two years, he learned to be in control of his emotions, and he no longer yells and verbally abuses his family. He is now able to experience new relationships with his wife and children. He is happier, and his vibrations are so different that he is able to have peaceful relationships with his co-workers as well.

Chapter 3 -
The Rays of Divinity

Our challenging times bring transformation of consciousness through the incoming energy of Sirius, the Great Bear and the constellation of Aquarius.The year 2025 will also bring transformation on Earth. This time it will come through the incoming Fourth Ray of Divinity—the Ray of Harmony through Conflict. We live in a sea of energy and the seven Rays of divinity are its currents. These seven Rays are the seven qualities through which the one life, the Creator, expresses itself. The seven energies create forms, meaning of life, and cosmic laws, pushing everything toward evolution. They are the builders of the universe. The seven Rays have continuously passed in and out of manifestation upon the earth and have left their mark on mankind down through the ages. Everything in our solar system is under the influence of a particular Ray—every planet, every kingdom in nature, and every individual. These Rays, when better known, will become the base of the science of psychology in the future.

Alice Bailey gave us the following understanding for the influence of the seven Rays.

The first three are the major Rays:

RAY 1 is the energy of will and power, also called the Will of God. This Ray works both as a builder and as a destroyer, bringing cycles to an end in order to build anew. People benefit from the energy of Ray 1 when they dissolve outdated beliefs and patterns in order to progress, or when initiating new ideas. In its positive aspect, Ray 1 is the will to do good; on its negative pole, it can bring tyranny, whether in a household or a nation.

RAY 2 is the energy of love and wisdom, also called the Love of God. It is the attractive force in the universe and the basis for the law of attraction; it creates all life. Ray 2 is the dominant Ray in our solar system. As individuals, we express Ray 2 as love, compassion, or wisdom in its positive pole, or self indulgence and laziness in its negative aspect.

RAY 3 is the energy of active intelligence, also called the Mind of God. It organizes all life. By producing synthesis in the physical plane, it brings the power to manifest and to evolve. People influenced by Ray 3 are often involved in business and finance, creating good or evil in those areas, using their remarkable intelligence either to manipulate others or to help them create better life conditions.

The following four Rays are "sub-rays" of the Ray 3, or Rays of attribute:

RAY 4 is the energy of harmony, beauty, and art. It is also the energy of harmony through conflict. It is the dual aspect of desire, revealing the path to higher consciousness. In its duality, Ray 4 first brings us the strength to fight and then the desire not to fight any longer and to reach peaceful cooperation. Humanity as a whole evolves under Ray 4, pushing us toward the beauty and harmony of the soul.

RAY 5 is the energy of concrete knowledge and science. It brings revelation and understanding to the mind. It is the revealer of truth. People under its influence often participate in research because of their great accuracy and attention to detail. In the positive aspect, such focus allows the piercing of the veil and the reaching of the soul; in the negative pole, the need for details and accuracy prevents one from expanding beyond the proven to the unknown.

RAY 6 is the energy of devotion, idealism, and sacrifice. It brings vision and the determination to follow it all the way without discrimination—often, unfortunately, to the exclusion of other people's beliefs and ideas. On the positive aspect, we find spiritual, loving people devoted to helping others; on the negative aspect, we find narrow-minded people incapable of seeing any other point of view but their own.

RAY 7 is the energy of ceremonial magic and order. It brings the descent of higher consciousness into matter. In its positive aspect, it leads humanity to mental freedom, loving understanding, and spiritual aspiration. In its negative aspect, it brings materialism through its ability to manifest.

The year 2025 will be the dawn of great evolution in all consciousness, with the coming of the Fourth Ray of Divinity in 2025. We will see transformation in the ideologies held by the human race. Many people by then will perceive subtle energies we call the "aura." More people will be described as clairvoyant, or intuitive. There will be an overwhelming number of encounters with "the other side" on the astral plane due to the thinning of the veil. Great perception of truth concerning what we call death will challenge our way of thinking. The stimulation of the mind will generate research in areas such as the subtle, unseen energetic bodies and will lead to the scientific study of the existence of the soul. By 2025, many will be on the path. We will regard many of our activities of today as barbaric and un-evolved, much as we now regard aspects of life at the turn of the twentieth century. People were dying of tuberculosis, planes had not been invented, and communication was conducted through postal mail. The evolution that occurs over the next twenty years will be comparable to the evolution of the last one hundred years.

Of course, every period has its problems. Energy is always expressed simultaneously on positive and negative lines of force. If humanity evolves in consciousness, it is the consciousness itself that will be transformed, and not just in the way we physically transport ourselves from one place to another, or through the medical breakthroughs that will lead to the healing of formerly incurable diseases. As humanity raises its consciousness toward the soul, it will interrupt the projection of lower forms of emotions, such as fear, therefore stopping the production of darkness. When we bring in the light and open our hearts to soul expression, we transform the negative pole of our energy and find the balance between the two great lines of forces—the darkness and the light. This is what the Fourth Ray of Divinity will come here to guide us through. We will be called to reach harmony through conflicts and to find the balance that will allow us to experience peace and beauty.

The Universe, therefore God, is helping us by presenting this energy to us. We need to regard it as a gift, to embrace it and grow from it. No matter how difficult growing may seem, remember that we are helped, supported, and loved unconditionally. God is love. No matter the name of your God, no matter whether or not you believe there is one—you live in this consciousness, whose essence is love. So let's elevate ourselves to feel it and to bring down its vibrations for others to benefit from it too. Witness the wonders of nature, the multiple miracles of every day life we do not even pay attention to anymore. It is time to refocus our attention on what we want, instead of creating by default, and remaining unaware of our thoughts patterns and direction of the mind. Pay attention to where your intention and thoughts are, as this is what you will experience.

Chapter 4 -
The Evolution Of Humanity

For eons, humanity has evolved through trial and error. Good and bad karmas have been accumulating. All of this energy has been put into motion and needs to be played out. We are now called to transform this energy and make new choices as it surfaces.

At the dawn of time, evolution was very slow; it was only when our mind began to develop that evolution accelerated. As the pace of evolution continues to accelerate and our minds continue to grow, changes will come faster and faster. The past one hundred years has seen a growth in progress that is unparalleled in the preceding thousand years. A transformation similar to what took place in the last century can be achieved in the next twenty-five years.

Humanity has evolved through time in what are called "root races." The first root race to experience life in physical bodies was the Lemurians. Lemurians had heightened emotions and a focus on survival; they were human, yet that race could be considered animal/man. The Atlanteans succeeded the Lemurians; they experienced the beginnings of mental development. Our present race is called the Aryan, which should not be confused with the misuse of the word by Hitler during WWII. The purpose of our root race is to perfect the mind, rising from our lower mind to our higher, or abstract, mind. The next coming root race will bring the complete dissolution of the veil that separates our personality from our divine self, resulting in the merging of our soul with our personality.

The first acceleration of evolution was experienced by the Atlanteans. Much information regarding the secret teachings was given to the people at that time by the more advanced souls, forming what is called the Hierarchy of the planet. This information was given in order to help the mind develop with greater speed, thus raising the consciousness of humanity. This, however, did not result in the expected outcome because of the lack of spiritual development in the personalities. They misused the information—the power given was used for selfish, materialistic, individual purposes—resulting in negative karma for both humanity and the Hierarchy. A lot of people turned toward thievery; greed and abuse of power were more and more prominent. A large number of souls accrued great losses in evolutionary development by using the sacred knowledge given by the Hierarchy, in service to the selfish purposes of the personality. The subsequent black magic generated much negative karma, greatly delaying the progress of the souls' evolution and resulted in the requirement of additional difficult incarnations.

Since then, the Hierarchy has had to take a stand, retreating from its direct involvement with the incarnated personalities. Their participation is now mostly conducted through soul contact. It is a safer approach, as it requires individuals to raise their consciousness to soul level before they can be trusted with higher power. It also leaves humanity to its own deeds and to the consequences brought about from interaction with each other, either as individuals or as nations. This subsequent period has been called the period of the Kali Yuga, or the Dark Age. We are arriving at the end of this period and its critical year of 2012.

In Atlantean times, the Hierarchy physically interacted with humanity. Some of its members incarnated on Earth in order to create spiritual temples and teach scientific knowledge, based on vibrational resonance, such as sound and color. Through that knowledge, people could manifest at will. This ability to manifest, which was supposed to bring peace and happiness and eradicate fear of lack, instead resulted in a civilization of materialism. These tools were used for selfish purposes rather than for the benefit of all. The dark forces were winning. More people were empowering their personalities, rather than opening to higher consciousness through gratitude and love. As a result, that civilization had to be removed from the earth and its continent destroyed, in order to save humanity from the fall into darkness. This is why so many cultures have the legend of the flood.

The perfecting of our personality and the elevation of our vibrations to higher consciousness is now required before we can be trusted again with higher power. This will happen steadily, with the evolution of the mind of humanity through the tool of education. More and more people are able to use critical thinking. This will eventually lead them to question their life and purpose, and in this process contact their higher or abstract mind to apprehend greater truth. This process is only a vibratory process, and it is accelerated by the infiltration of light through the veil of distortion, which we call "the astral plane." The astral plane is composed of all the thoughts and emotions of humanity and separates the higher consciousness or soul vibration from the personality. It creates a false feeling of separateness, as the mind is dualistic and separative in nature, while the soul is uniting. The mind is thought; the soul is love. Love is the basis of the law of attraction; therefore, the soul attracts and unites.

The few who escaped the destruction of the continent of Atlantis became the seed for the transfer of knowledge in several more-developed ancient civilizations. This knowledge was based on science, geometry, and astrology, and we can see this influence distinctly through the Egyptian and Mayan civilizations. The advancement of those civilizations reached their peak once that knowledge was imparted and used. Yet, again, the development of consciousness was not sufficient enough to sustain the continuous progress that would enable the societies to thrive through that knowledge. So as it is in nature when expansion is no longer possible, those civilizations died. It is the law of cycles—evolution and involution, or the destruction of what once was. It applies to everything in creation, from an atom to a human being to a planet. The cycle of creation goes through a birth, or spring; a striving period, or summer; a declining, or autumn; and a death, or winter. These are the cycles that all lives go through, in shorter or longer periods of time, but in constant and immutable cycles.

After the decline of ancient civilizations came the period of evolution through Christianity. This cycle was under the Sixth Ray of Divinity, or the energy of Devotion and Idealism. Like all energy, the Sixth Ray has both a positive and a negative aspect. This Ray is expressed in its positive or in its negative aspect depending on the level of evolution of the consciousness of the one it touches. Energy is neutral until it encounters a consciousness, human or other, who will use it according to its level of development.

So under the 2300 year cycle of this Ray, we have seen the best and the worst in humanity's creations, and its reaction to events or circumstances. In the positive aspect we have the saints, who sacrificed their lives with compassion and devotion for the good of the whole to assist humanity. On the negative aspect we had the wars of religion—destruction in the name of God—where people imposed their views and beliefs on others for the purpose of their devotion and idealism. The crystallization of this energy made them intolerant and spiritually blind, responding only to their personality strivings and desires. This phase of evolution was under the astrological sign of Pisces, so we call it the Piscean Age.

Since 1675, however, another Ray has made its appearance. It will remain in effect for the next two thousand years. It is the Seventh Ray of Divinity, or the Ray of Order and Magic. This energy, combined with the new astrological sign of Aquarius (which the earth is now entering) is having an entirely different influence on humanity. It is responsible for the rise in consciousness and the new phase of development that we call the New Age, or Aquarian Age. This New Age is calling for a new form of spirituality and once again for evolution of consciousness. The Seventh Ray is the energy that will bring Spirit into matter, or the higher vibration of the soul into the personality. This will allow us to live our cycles of physical incarnation under the influence of and with the participation of the soul, producing unity among humankind and heightening the sense of compassion for all life.

Ray 7 was the Ray of influence at the time of the destruction of Atlantis. Because this Ray is also the energy that brings physical manifestation, most everyone today can witness the result of their thought projections, by the physical manifestation that follows—often rather quickly. It has become a platitude to say that energy follows thought, but with the Ray 7, now in activity around the earth, creation through thoughts will happen ever faster as this ray gains in power. On the positive aspect of this Ray, Spirit will be brought down to be manifested on Earth; on the negative aspect, materialism through selfishness will also be on the rise. It will also bring about instant karmas, both good and bad. Though the Atlanteans failed to elevate their consciousness under this Ray, the mind of humanity is more evolved today, particularly in the developed countries, due largely to their emphasis on education. Additionally, the new generations now in incarnation are also more evolved than people of the past. It is the hope of the Hierarchy that the idealism that has been created under Ray 6 and which is now part of the astral plane will be brought down by Ray 7 to the physical plane, causing the heart of humanity to open. Through this opening, we will increase the expression of our divine self or soul consciousness.

At this time, both Ray 6 and Ray 7 are in effect, though Ray 6 is slowly phasing out and Ray 7 is not yet in full force. However, nothing can stop the progression of Ray 7 and the disappearance of Ray 6 any more than we can stop time. Humanity is accountable for its response to these energies. As larger numbers of people invoke the soul consciousness, the more the Hierarchy will respond. They will not interfere in our creations unless we call on them and invoke their help. We are not working alone. The Hierarchy is working with us through our souls, and we can feel this connection as we raise our vibrations. Light will always dissolve darkness, even in the troubled times we are experiencing now. The more we invoke the light, the easier the transition will be.

Leaving behind the Dark Age should be viewed as progress and liberation, not as a dreadful time. Even though the light disturbs many non-evolved forms, the resistance and reaction it creates will be short lived. The stronger the intensity of the light, the faster those non-evolved consciousnesses will be transformed and elevated. When we stop drawing on lower emotions, such as fear and jealousy, love and unity will be more prevalent in our daily life.

Along the way, death in the name of God has been experienced everywhere. Today again, division is generated in the name of God, along with idealistic thoughts of what God is. Religions have sprung up everywhere, bringing more division and separation among mankind than any other ideology. All this is based on emotional impulses and the separation created by our mind. Personality conflicts will stop as we rise to our hearts and experience the true love that comes from unity with our soul.

From the Atlantean race to the present, life has been experienced through the division of the mind. Unity will come with the new root race. Our children are the embryo of that race. Humanity will rise to the higher mind level, reaching the soul. From that vantage point, the desire to help the less fortunate and to educate and lift the spirit of many will dominate. The Hierarchy has watched our evolution and is illuminating some great minds.

The Renaissance and the development of the arts emerged from the period of darkness experienced during the Middle Ages and the crusades. The many great philosophers throughout Europe followed, adding to the great philosophies of the ancient Greeks. According to the law of cycles, civilizations rise and disappear, always to form again, greater and renewed. From one continent to another, from one civilization to another, the rise of power has led to the loss of spirit, bringing the death and eventually the disappearance of those civilizations. There is no life without spirit. When one loses its spirit, the process of death starts. Death is a time of purification. For an individual, a nation, or a civilization, the process is the same: the positive and enlightened energy is retrieved by the soul, and the negative or darkness is reabsorbed by the earth. This process will go on until all is light and the earth has become a sacred planet—when only the life of the spirit will inhabit the earth and physical life will have been purified.

Chapter 5 -
The Life Cycles

Every incarnated consciousness goes through cycles of growth and development, during which a new level of consciousness is reached and a change in life is often experienced. As far as humanity is concerned, these cycles happen every nine years. During the first three years of the nine-year cycle, we plant seeds. The following four years, we reap what we have sown, and the last two years we let go of all that will not follow us in the next cycle.

During these cycles are peaks of development: at age thirty-six, when the personality matures; at age forty-five, when we are often pushed into new paths or rededication of the Self; and at age fifty, when we go through our "Chiron" return. Chiron, for the astrologers, is the symbol of the wounded healer. It takes exactly fifty years for Chiron to come back to the place it had been at the time of one's birth. Chiron's energy pushes us to review our life, and our life's purpose. Some decide to take action to heal the wounds inflicted during the first fifty years of their life and then move forward with renewed strength and wisdom. This healing brings more joy and happiness in the second part of their life, as they are enriched by the knowledge of their experiences but free from the pain that was attached to them. The ones who are too trapped in personality conflicts might give up and not be able to look at life with new hopes and expectations. Their spirit is slowly moving out, and they see their life as in the past. A number of very successful men and women have created their fortune after the age of fifty. The colonel with Kentucky Fried Chicken (now KFC) is an example of this pattern, as well as Bill Gates, who chose to donate a great portion of his fortune at the age of fifty.

The year 2012 stands at the close of a transformative cycle for the earth. These cycles are of a much greater span of time for the earth than for us human beings, of course. The end of this Dark Age period is a major transformative process, healing for the earth and all that live upon it. We are part of this transformation, as it touches all of us and awaits our reaction and participation.

We often think that life events are just "happening" to us without real involvement or influence on our part—"It just is"—and it appears as if we do not have any power or say so over it, no control over our circumstances. We often think that life events just happen to us. This perception, however, is not the truth. Our life is but the representation of our state of mind. Our experiences have been and are created through our own thoughts and intents. There is nothing that comes to us that we have not opened ourselves to in our present life or in a previous one. Therefore, we are susceptible to our own karmas and the karma of the groups we associate with. Because of the power of our thought, we are also at the mercy of the karma created by our thoughts, and not just by our past actions.

Ultimately, humanity as a whole is under the same larger group karma and on the same progressive path. We are creating this path as we go along, and it is a mistake to believe that all we need to be concerned with is our own life. Everything that is happening all around the earth concerns us. Energy is moved by the thoughts, emotions, and actions of everyone, and in turn, these thoughts, emotions, and actions are experienced by all. The darkness generated by the wars, by the oppression of slavery, in every country throughout the ages, is now coming to the surface to be purified and transformed. Each of us might not have participated in all the wars of the past, but we are here on Earth at this time to interact with those energies and transform them, purifying them as they enter our mind or our emotional body. Some of us may think we are without prejudice; those will be pushed to experience some form of prejudice purposely. Facing one's prejudices will lead us to make choices and hopefully purify those thoughts and emotions arising in our consciousness. This is our role as evolved human beings: to be the liberators of the energies created by humanity down through the ages.

What is the benefit of choosing to participate in this cleanup time? The benefit of this work is the creation of good karma, great spiritual advancement, development of our individual personality, and that of humanity as a whole. In doing this, we are creating a better world, not only for our children but also for ourselves, as we will come back to inhabit the earth again in future incarnations. With this in mind, we might ponder on the kind of world we want to live in, and what we want to experience when we incarnate again. The impact of our choices has never been more relevant; we are creating not just for this present life, but for many to come. There is a continuity of life. Life is energy. No one can kill energy. Energy will take shape into form again and again. What these forms will be depends on the quality of the energy behind them. For this we are responsible. The quality of our thoughts will determine the level of refinement of the forms created. We are the ones with a thinking mind, and through our thoughts, we are taking part in creation. Therefore, we must deliberately consider the kind of world we want to live in now and in the future, and act accordingly to produce it, as our everyday choices always determine our future, either for our present life or for our next incarnation. For instance, we may have great intentions about refraining from negative speech about others but may revert to it out of unhealthy curiosity or insecurity. The need to set ourselves apart from the group also leads to the unconscious participation in gossip.

In addition to the karma created by humanity, there are cosmic preceding factors to this age of transition that have determined the level of evolution of all the consciousness upon the earth. The handicaps presented by previous cosmic circumstances, independent of us and out of our control, are called "inherited circumstances" to life on Earth. These circumstances have certainly slowed down the advancement of the expression of light in the consciousness of this planet, affecting human, devic, and all other lives and consciousness on Earth. From this impediment, we will acquire a richer, more profound experience and expression of love as we slowly progress. Every difficulty presents us with a choice between love and hatred. Every challenge makes us weaker or stronger; every pain allows us to reach upward to our soul for relief or downward toward resentment and anger. And even though the progress is slower because of all those inherited circumstances that create such duality in our earth experience, they allow our individual consciousness, and therefore the consciousness of God, in whom we live, to become richer and deeper in its expression of love. We gain the understanding and compassion that only pain and hardship allow us to open to, once we choose to comprehend the purpose of these difficulties and move into the light. Without this duality, we would not be able to appreciate the beauty of the peace and serenity we experience once we open to the light and choose it consistently.

We have chosen to evolve upon a planet that is affected by the sun and the moon. The moon is a decaying planet that releases its non-evolved, unperfected consciousness to the earth. The sun is the source of all life, evolution, and purification. From a dead animal's body in the wild, to our own body when we are outside, the sun purifies all energy, including a congested, stagnant energy in our own energy field. Our role as humanity is to transmute the non-evolved energy or darkness into the evolved form of the light. We are doing so through our own development of consciousness and mental evolution. We are the transformers. We are aided in this task through the energy we receive from the more evolved planets in our solar system, which we call the "sacred planets," as well as by the purifying and revitalizing energy of the sun.

Chapter 6 -
Evolution Beyond 2025

We are approaching a time when life will have a very different outlook, and when we will witness various events happening upon the earth. This should not be feared or resisted but embraced, as it represents a much needed change through the evolution of mankind and will bring an enhanced quality of life for everyone. Before this transition is complete though, we will witness loss of lives due to the earth's transformation. And if we experience fear and insecurity in most countries, it is for the purpose that as we grow out of these fears, we will be able to reach higher to our soul.

When there is no longer a sense of security in our world, when everything seems out of control, there is always a renewed faith. It is unfortunate that we often need to experience fear or distress as an incentive to look above and reach higher. When the personality feels in charge and controls its world, there is not much of an impulse to reach toward a higher purpose and our greater self. However, when we feel unsettled and out of control, having hit rock bottom, the only way to look is up. It is like a child experiencing his world, becoming strong in his independence, but then turning back to his parents when he feels scared. So it is also the reaction of humanity, when discomfort and pain challenge its physical reality.

Remember, we are never alone; there is support and guidance all along the way from our own Higher Self and soul, as well as from our "guides," the beings who evolved before us. We simply need to ask; we just need to invoke help and guidance in order to receive it. As the material world and its institutions crumble around us, higher values—brotherhood, acceptance, cooperation, and compassion—will surface in the mind and heart of humanity. The new race will emerge from new generations, composed of more advanced souls who will incarnate in order to bring more wisdom and knowledge of greater value to humanity.

We can already see the emergence of this new race through the children known as "the Indigo Children." These children are "old" beings whose souls have evolved beyond average human development because they have had more incarnations. They represent the externalization of the Hierarchy, or the appearance of the Hierarchy of evolved souls on Earth. They have been coming in larger numbers since the World War II generation, and they will come in greater numbers to every land and every race in order to elevate the consciousness of humanity, and they will guide us in our evolution. With this happening, we will see much transformation in all fields of work, not only from the philosophic and spiritual aspect, but in the organization of life itself—through our institutions and governments.

Some of these advanced souls can be recognized as children, exhibiting powerful intuitive and sensory abilities. An example of this is of a little girl in kindergarten, who said to her mother one day, "I don't want to go to school today. I'm tired of seeing rainbows. Rainbows around Mrs. Smith, rainbows around Billy, rainbows around Kelly . . ." This little girl could see auras around people, and because of the variety of colors, she referred to them as rainbows.

Too much emphasis is given today to materialism and possession. The world is directed by the few who unleash and enslave the rest of humanity for their own benefit, gain, and power. They sacrifice the lives and wellbeing of others out of greed and thirst for power. This will change, as humanity retrieves its clear vision and turns its consciousness away from materialism and individuality to experience the joy of community and of helping others and being supported by others. Then we will realize that we have the power to create our reality by involving the love and unity of the soul, rather than succumbing to the fears and separateness generated by our personalities, when we feel isolated and divided. We will understand the strength that comes from community and group support, and most importantly, we will have the drive to act upon those realizations and build sustainable communities.

We often believe we need to be poor in order to be spiritual. This is not so. This is a belief created in and strengthened by repeated past lives under the Christianity influence, which most of us are holding in our cellular memory. Most of us have incarnated as Christian in one life or another, and consequently resonate with this belief that we need to be poor, even if we are not of this faith today. It is time to release this false and outdated belief, especially when we realize how much wealth was accumulated during that time by the ones imparting those beliefs to humanity.

Money is but an energy that circulates—or should circulate, as all energy does. What renders money "evil" is the blocking of its flow. We horde money out of fear of not having enough, and then we horde more out of greed and give so much value to money that we are willing to do anything to have more. Money then becomes a poisonous gift; the more we have, the more we fear losing it. Because of the law of karma, if it is not acquired honestly, we, in fact, often lose it. We project so much fear and envy around money that we trap this energy in lower levels of consciousness, and then we say "money is evil." Money is not evil, but what we do with it often is. We need to regard money as we should regard all energy—with respect and gratitude. When money is used for the greater good of all, rather than for selfish purposes, this energy will be rendered positive and will flow with great amplitude, simply because it will be empowered by love.

The law of attraction is generated by the Second Ray of Divinity, the Ray of Love and Wisdom. This Ray is the energy that brings molecules and atoms together in order to create physical life and create forms. When we use money with appreciation and gratitude, we energize it with soul energy. It comes back to us multiplied. Remember the old adage of tithing: all that you give will come back to you tenfold. Giving with generosity to help others does not mean we will become poor. To the contrary: as we change the energy of money through the use of gratitude, rather than love for money itself, we render this energy positive, and we multiply it. However, the impulse to give needs to come with sincerity from the heart, with the sheer intention of giving, not with the purpose of return. If we give just out of the intention of receiving more, there is no involvement of the heart quality, but only the selfishness of the personality. Give of your resources as it feels comfortable, in an act of love and generosity. If you do not have financial resources, give of yourself, your time, your knowledge, your gifts. All you give will come back to you a hundredfold.

The fastest way to dissolve bad karma is to create good karma, which dissolves the negative. Through service, the personality changes, and the energy of the soul comes closer and closer until it finally illuminates the whole consciousness of the individual, fully empowering its personality. Often people fear that releasing control and trusting their Higher Self means losing power, when in fact it increases the abilities of our personality. By strengthening the connection with our Higher Self, we receive more tools and insights to maneuver in our physical world.

This elevation of consciousness concerning money and resources is inevitable as it is necessary for our growth. It will be facilitated by the arrival of the new, more advanced souls in the domain of finance. We already have a few enlightened personalities giving most of their fortune to help the populations of underdeveloped countries. They parallel and hopefully one day will offset the personalities of the ones who work from the darker, un-evolved side, who take advantage of those underdeveloped countries to rob them of their resources. Both light and dark are present. We often believe we are working for the side of good, especially when we look at the outpouring of aid to less developed countries, after they experience a natural disaster. Yet while we are moved into action as a nation by such events, we also mostly consider our own personal needs, such as when we choose to continue promoting the use of gas-burning automobiles that cause more pollution than they should at the expense of the environment.

Yet nothing will stop the development of the consciousness of humanity; the march is on. We can stall it for a very long time by resisting change, or out of fear of losing our illusory security, or we can speed up this evolution through greater understanding and generosity. In any case, we cannot stop evolution any more than we can stop time.

As the world economy crumbles, it will transform into a more solid, real value system. Barter will eventually be restored, and money in all countries will lose its value. New, universal modes of exchange will be created, and fair exchange of resources will be established among nations. With time, humanity will realize that all human beings are part of the same soul, the same origin, and that what is done to one is done to all. With a more balanced and equitable appropriation of money, more value will be given to lives. This will take time, of course, but world events will speed up the awakening.

The incoming Fourth Ray of Divinity, the energy of Harmony through Conflict, in 2025 will push humanity toward the development of consciousness. Through this quality of harmony through conflict, the energy of this Ray will generate difficulties around the world in order to push humanity toward the desire for peace and eventually to achieve harmony. It will push us in our spiritual development, as harmony can only be found through unity, and unity is the quality found in the soul. The year 2025 will be the beginning of a great evolution toward harmony and will bring to humanity a much-needed period of peace.

Before we reach 2025, many changes will take place. The influx of higher light vibrations will disrupt darkness, and this will create a lot of resistance in the human consciousness. Because light activates darkness before it dissolves it, we will see the rise of anger and intolerance among humanity and nations. We will see the disruption of the economy and destruction through aggression. This will be due to the resistance to change in the emotional and the mental levels of human consciousness. We can see this in ourselves as we step onto the path; we can recognize this in others and have compassion for them.

On the individual level as well as the macro-level, this transition can be made easier by the increasing number of people who invoke light. Invoking light is not the same as praying. Often, one prays with great hope that his prayers will be answered. Bringing the light is being an active participant in the transformation of the energy in order to elevate its vibrations. The higher the vibration of the light we are bringing down, the faster the dissolution of the darkness takes place, thus eliminating the resistance we would otherwise encounter. This bringing of the light is not about destroying darkness or un-evolved forms; it is about transforming them and helping them evolve, bringing these vibrations to a higher level of consciousness. The bringing of the light is the work of every one of us, in this crucial time of development for humanity. How do we do this? By healing ourselves, controlling our own emotions and negative thoughts, and bringing the light to our fear, anger, or resentment when they surface. Bringing the light systematically to those emotions or thoughts, every time, will chip away at them little by little, transforming our consciousness. We can bring light to our darker emotions by sending a jolt of white light into them when they surface, or simply by asking our Higher Self to dissolve them.

As we move through this time of transformation, many people will decide to leave their physical body and serve instead from the other side, the astral plane of the earth. This level is composed of all the thoughts and feelings of humanity. We all interact with, and are influenced by, the thoughts and feelings composing the consciousness of this plane. We can easily see the potency of the astral plane when, for example, a trend or fashion takes a particular group of the population by storm. Some of us are more needed in the astral plane to balance the energies there than in the physical plane when action and destruction are happening. There is a real need for transformation and balance to occur in the astral plane before the energy descends and affects the physical plane. It is of great concern when emotions become so out of control that they unleash their force and affect the actions and reactions of humanity.

Therefore, a number of us will decide to continue our service from the astral plane level, minimizing the effect of fears and anger that will be generated. This transition of lives from one level to another is to be regarded as useful and beneficial rather than painful and dramatic. Remember, death does not exist. When death of the physical body occurs, it is simply the release of the soul from the form, and the elevation of consciousness to another plane. The freedom experienced by the soul—which is who we really are—allows us to perceive a greater truth and participate in the stabilization and expansion of another level of consciousness, before our next descent and reincarnation in the physical plane. The more we understand the necessity and the use of the work done on different levels of consciousness, the easier it will be to accept the losses of human lives on the physical plane. Not everyone will leave the physical plane in order to help on another level, but many will. Others will simply reach the normal ending of their cycle of life, when the soul withdraws because it has learned everything possible to be learnt from the present incarnation, and when the mind becomes crystallized with age and cannot progress any further. Some will not be able to sustain the new vibrations in their physical bodies and will become sick. Others will decide to sacrifice their lives and will benefit in their next incarnation from the accumulation of good karma. All will live either in or out of the body, and transformation of the human consciousness will benefit from this unique and special time.

As time passes, we will see more and more people change and transform their thoughts, ideas, and understanding. They will turn to greater values, realizing that material values bring only ephemeral comfort and satisfaction. As the world economy deteriorates, people who found security in possessions will realize that this security was only an illusion. Those who try to control their world and other people will realize that their power is not a match with the ultimate power of the creator. With time will come the necessary transformation for the advancement of humanity as a whole.

What lies beyond this is the establishing of a new order in human life. People will come to understand that karma makes one always catch up with one's actions. Domination by the few to the detriment of others will disappear little by little and will be replaced by true leadership. It will be a world in which politicians will care for people and will apply themselves to serve for the benefit of all, rather than for their own career. As consciousness elevates, it is inevitable that truth will be revealed. Information will surface regarding particular individuals and their actions. This will force others to examine their own behaviors as corruption is brought into the open. This also includes the media, which suppresses information out of fear or for gain. The public will be made aware of what has been suppressed until now, thus forcing changes in our institutions.

To navigate this transformation, it will be helpful to remember that the events precipitated by our challenging times are here to help transform human consciousness and behaviors, not as retribution. Doing the work of clearing the astral plane or our emotional body will help keep emotions under control, calming fear and anger as this process of transformation unfolds. There are more and more advanced people walking the earth today, who help in the transformation. Some are already part of the incoming, more advanced beings we call the Hierarchy; they are here to help humanity through this time of transition. They are present in all areas of work and affect the consciousness of everyone in their surroundings. Some of these people will be our leaders of tomorrow in all departments of human affairs. But remember, we cannot rely on them only. It is the responsibility of everyone to participate, to recognize them and help them do the work they came here to do. Here is where difficulties may arise. Transformation will happen through chaos if we continue to cherish the old erroneous material values, following charismatic leaders who prey on our emotions, rather than choosing more genuine leaders, devoid of empty promises, who demonstrate real care and responsibility for governance.

Transformation is inevitable. It is put in motion by cosmic intent, way beyond our control; our time is a benchmark in this transformation, it is part of the astrology of the earth, resulting in cosmic alignment. The rise of the human mind is both the goal and the means for this transformation. The quicker we adapt and evolve, the more harmonious this transition will be. Education in all forms is a key component. Advancement comes through the ability to think and resonate. It allows us to get out of our illusions and the lies we are fed. The more educated we become, the more we produce advanced thoughts. As we develop the ability to use discrimination and discernment we will have a clearer perception of truth and will make better decisions. A supporting fact here is the "Flynn effect," discovered in 1999, which says that the average IQ of entire nations has risen over the decades, as more people have become better educated and enjoy a better quality of health.

Between 2012 and 2025, we will see the rise of spiritual teachers and the decline of materialistic values. People incarnated at that time will prepare us for the real elevation of consciousness. This will be an exciting time as it will elevate humanity to a greater position of unity. Humanity is part of the great tapestry of energy forming the etheric body of the earth. It is important to understand this in order to realize how intricately connected we all are. The pain of one becomes the pain of all others; the joy of one is shared in the same way by all others. In the web of energy forming this tapestry we also connect with all other forms of life, seen and unseen.

Chapter 7 -
Who are We?

We are multidimensional beings. We have multiple experiences simultaneously at different levels of consciousness. What we term the "personality" is comprised of a physical body, an emotional body, and a mental body. These different parts are composed of aggregates of atoms that become individual consciousnesses on every level.

The physical body is easy to identify. Around the physical body is the etheric, or energy body. This level is the great pathway through which the energy from all the levels, including the energy from the soul, enters the physical body. Our physical health and well-being is directly affected by the vitality, depletion, or congestion of our etheric body.

The next level is the emotional, or astral body. In psychology, we call the consciousness of that level the "inner child"; it forms part of our subconscious. On the astral level, our emotions mingle with and can be influenced by the emotions of other people. This is why we sometimes have feelings that cannot be explained by our life circumstances. It is also why we can sometimes be more reactive to people around us than we consciously want to be. As it is part of our subconscious mind, we are not consciously aware of all its activity, yet it affects our daily life, as we often find ourselves in states of being we have difficulty controlling.

The next level is the most evolved of our personality, our lower "concrete" mind. Psychology refers to this as the ego. It is not divine, as it is not connected yet to our higher mind, the part of our divine self which connects us to our soul. In our mental body, we formulate and receive thoughts, we influence others, we even communicate telepathically—such as when partners say the same thing at the same time, or when close friends have an urge to call each other at the same moment. From that level we create good or evil, using its creativity and intelligence to energize either side. We create thought forms that vibrate in our energy fields and influence our emotional state as well as our physical health and what we attract or manifest.

The consciousnesses in those three levels are called "devas" and "elementals." They are affected by the thoughts and emotions we choose to energize. They evolve alongside us and are the direct recipients either of the soul energy or of the darkness we bring to them when we create thoughts motivated by fears. They interact with the energy fields of others around us, but also with the devas and elementals of nature, the air, the plants, the water, and the earth. Therefore, the quality of our own energy field affects and is affected by everything and everyone around us.

For example, the quality of the air where we live affects the devas and elementals of our energy fields, and in turn, the quality of our thoughts affects the devas and elementals of our environment. We are interdependent with all. This tapestry is part of the body of God. We affect it by the quality of our thoughts and actions in the same way that the cells in our body affect our health. If we get sick, our body reacts by disrupting our bodily functions and creating fever.

We play a parallel role in the body of God. Our thoughts and resulting actions over the ages have created a need for purification. Our resistance will create more illness and disruption. Our thoughts and actions in harmony with the law of creation will bring back health and order in that body, and therefore in our surroundings. Purging will happen, and harmony will be restored. This purging is independent of which God we worship but is dependent on how we live our lives. Do we demonstrate kindness and care toward others, or are our actions driven by selfishness? This is the key factor for the law of karma—the law of cause and effect. The way we affect others is also the way we affect the body of God. Everyone needs to do some level of introspection. Everyone can change something in their way of living, in their behavior. There is always room for improvement, no matter where we are on the ladder of evolution.

Another important thing we need to understand about ourselves, which will help us evolve to the level of the soul, is the concept of the two different main energies that are present in our personality. These are our male and our female principles, or the male self and the female self.

The male energy is on the right side of our body, and the female energy is on the left. You can corroborate this by taking a photo of yourself and cutting it in half. If you make a mirror image of each side and put together two left sides or two right sides, the resulting image will not look like you. The left and right side of your face do not look exactly alike. These two sides are a representation of two very different energies held in our subconscious mind.

Our male self carries the energy of strength, power, and sometimes aggression. We use it to survive, physically or emotionally, to fight our way through life. It is more related to our personality needs.

Our female self energy is one of love and innate intuition. It is the energy that will eventually connect us with our soul through the law of attraction, as soul is love. The difficulty is that our female self does not have the strength or self-assurance to reach the height needed to reach the soul. This part of us is more delicate, sensitive; she needs the male self to provide her with that strength. In turn, she will give him the love that will transform his willpower into will-to-good, and transform him from a warrior into a healer.

The male and female selves need to unite. As they come closer together, they will bring transformation in our mental, emotional, and etheric bodies, until unity is realized in all of those personality levels. This is a difficult task, as the two sides often do not see things in the same perspective and conflict with each other's desires. This is well illustrated by the "white and black angels" on our shoulders, the male self being more associated with the personality desires and the female self with the soul. Yet the development of consciousness requires that eventually we merge our male and female self energies, as once they are one, the personality becomes united on all levels and can now proceed with the integration of the soul. We cannot unite with the soul as long as our personality has not found unity between its physical, emotional, and mental selves. All those levels are part of our male and female selves, and the union of the two brings integration of all.

Some of us express more male energy or more female energy independently of our physical gender. Some women are very aggressive, like in business, for example, and work a lot from their male self-subconscious part. In turn, some men can be very sensitive and demonstrate a strong love and compassion coming from their female self-subconscious. The more humanity progresses in this development, the more we will see this happening. Male and female energies will be more noticeable in individual personality as they will express themselves independently from the physical gender. It should be our goal in our spiritual development to even out these two parts of ourselves so that as they merge, each will benefit from the qualities of the other, allowing us to achieve balance and unity in ourselves.

These challenging times call for *healing* and *unity* within all parts of ourselves in order to heal our emotions, elevate our minds, eliminate past negative karma, and create new positive karma. Living our life in harmony with nature, in all its expressions of life and with each other, is paramount. This requires altruism and respect for all. This requires growth and understanding. This requires one to want to better himself, and therefore, it requires effort and dedication. But the prize is great. It will result in peace and harmony, life without fear, and fulfillment through the opening of the heart. This might sound too good to be true, but it is not—it is simply a choice. You might wonder, "How do I do that?" One step at a time. You cannot change everything at once. And each step along the way brings more freedom, joy, and understanding and lays the groundwork for each succeeding step.

Start first by choosing to dissolve thoughts of anger and criticism when they arise in your consciousness by sending white light to them, and replace them with thoughts of gratitude for what you have or what you are learning. When you experience fear, ask your Higher Self to dissolve it and to surround you with grace, a golden light that will help you move through your fear. Choose to speak kind words, and do not participate when people denigrate others. Keep away from gossip and negative speech; they pollute your energy as much as they pollute the energy of the person you talk about. Negative speech ultimately pollutes the body of God in which we live. Practicing this simple yet difficult behavior pattern will change your life, and, eventually, the lives of people around you. Practice an act of kindness every day. Good, positive karmas will accumulate and erase bad, negative karmas. Free yourself from your past, either from this lifetime or from a previous one, by changing the patterns of your emotional body. Choose the thoughts you want to energize and bring into the light the ones that are wearing you down.

This is what this particular time of transformation is offering us: the ability to free and transform ourselves at a speed never offered before. How we choose to be part of this transformation is an individual choice, yet the greater the number of people choosing to take advantage of this opportunity, the faster and more profound the transformation will be. Everyone can participate. Everyone counts, no matter how large or how small the level of participation. We are all connected, and we all will benefit.

What we need to do is beyond actions; it starts with our thoughts. Our thoughts set energy in motion as concretely as our actions do. All creation starts with a thought. It is as true for the one we call God and his creation of the world as it is for us and the creation of our reality. Everything in the universe is created with the same attributes and templates, from the consciousness of the atom to the most advanced life. Sound moves the molecules (individual consciousnesses) through its resonance, precipitating physical forms or events in physical reality. We create and are subjected to many sounds in our daily life: the sound of our own voice, the words we speak that reflect our thoughts and make them manifest, the sound of the music we play, the television or radio programs we listen to. All have a direct effect on the devas and elementals in our own energy field. There are also sounds that we are less familiar with, such as the humming of electricity traveling at high speed along high voltage cables in every developed country. There is the sound of bombs we detonate in various parts of the world for wars or for testing. All those sounds affect the vibration of the energetic web we live in.

No one has a clear understanding of how those vibrations affect our mental, emotional, or physical body. No one has an understanding of how it might destroy some of the integrity of the energy field of the earth. This energy field acts also as a magnetic protective shield for all forms of life inhabiting it. No one has a real understanding of the transformation that results from those sounds or vibrations any more than we know or understand how medical treatments such as ultrasound or radiation affect the integrity of our energy field when we are subjected to them.

It is time for science to study, on a large scale, the possibility of the subtle energetic bodies. This would propel the science within the field of medicine toward incredible development and advancement and bring to humanity's awareness the interconnectedness we share with each other and our environment.

The many more advanced souls walking on Earth at this time are stimulating the mind of humanity. When we purify all the levels of our personality—physical, emotional, and mental—and their vibrations are raised, we will be able to connect our lower mind with our higher or abstract mind. Then our soul will have the ability to transmit information to our higher mind that will be captured by our brain. This will eventually result in telepathic communication with our soul. This soul connection will produce a greater download of information and understanding into the conscious level of the mind of humanity. It is expected that because of the new awareness created, humanity will respond and rise in large numbers to invoke additional help from the higher planes. The result will be the descent of light and love in our physical reality. This, in the Christian faith, is called "the return of the Christ," which is the descent of the soul into levels that our personality can reach. It is the divine consciousness from which we originate, and to which we are always connected. As we come into physical incarnation, we become denser in vibration, and as a result, few of us today can consciously connect with this "Christed" energy. This will change as humanity evolves.

The thoughts transmitted telepathically to humanity by more evolved beings (such as the Anteriens) are picked up by the most evolved, those who are able to raise their consciousness to a higher level. This information is given to eventually help in all realms of human activity, such as science and medicine, as much as psychology, philosophy, and spirituality. It is about the development of our mind in order to acquire greater truth and knowledge. From those seed thoughts, humanity will create and develop new realities, with the potential to be positive and negative in their applications. We see this too often when new discoveries fall into the wrong hands. This is why it is important that we develop spiritual consciousness along with the development of science, in all spheres of knowledge, so that we will not misuse the technology and power given. We are guarded and protected more than we think. Yet we walk a fine line, as we are also subjected to the law of cause and effect and to the law of evolution. We need to learn. We learn through our mistakes, and mistakes can be painful, yet we cannot escape advancement any more than we can escape karma.

Enlightenment is a state of being. It is achieved by quieting the mind in order to reach the alignment with the soul. In this alignment, there is only perfection, because while the mind is divisive, the soul is the unifier. When the mind becomes the tool for soul expression, all is light. Meditate on this and realize that the happenings precipitated and generated by this transition time are for the purpose of enlightenment, and therefore, there is always a deeper purpose behind all events, no matter how difficult some might be.

Chapter 8 –
Meditations

We cannot rise to the consciousness of the soul without practicing mediation. There are primarily two forms of meditation: transcendental and occult.

"Transcendental" is the form of meditation that has been practiced for thousands of years in the orient and is gaining popularity in the West. It consists of quieting the mind, focusing the mind's attention in the third eye, or Ajna center, and opening the heart though love while waiting for the soul to respond. This method of meditation takes long periods of time and often years of practice for the soul to turn its attention to the waiting personality, so the result is very slow. It has produced wonderful results for those who are patient and is a good method for people who are under Ray 6 and are therefore motivated by devotion.

"Occult" meditation is a more mental activity. The word "occult" simply refers to working with energy, though it sometimes has a negative connotation in our culture. In occult meditation, we use the creative imagination to move energy, building a scaffold in our energy field to reach the soul. This form of meditation is dynamic. It requires concentration, but because the lower mind remains active in its participation, there is less distraction and more efficiency.

A. Bailey also tells us in her book *Letters on Occult Meditation* that the people practicing transcendental meditation will have to eventually build the scaffolding in their energy field once the connection with soul is made, in order for the result to be permanent. Therefore, practicing occult meditation will give faster and more permanent results. Additionally, in these modern times, with the energy of so many people broadcasting and interacting with our mind, it is a little bit easier to focus using occult meditation, as our mind remains active.

Here is an example of how to practice occult meditation:
Sit in a quiet place, close your eyes, and take a couple of deep breaths to relax your body. In your mind's eye, visualize your chakra system, starting from the base of your spine going upward to your crown at the top of your head. As you move slowly along your spine, imagine your chakras moving clockwise and vibrating in unison and in harmony with each other. Because energy follows thought, this will automatically happen as you are visualizing it and intending the harmonization. Then imagine a cord of lighted energy linking your crown chakra to a ball of light above your head; this ball of light represents your soul. Allow your consciousness to rise along this cord and come closer to this light. With time you will come closer and closer to your soul. Eventually you can imagine yourself merging with this light. Let your Higher Self guide you in your progression, and do only what feels comfortable to you.

In any case, once you have made contact with your soul, either by coming closer or merging with it, through the power of the imagination, bring this light down along the lighted energy cord until it reaches your crown chakra and enters your body. Slowly bring it down to your third eye, then your throat and finally your heart. Once in your heart, make this light bigger and brighter.

Let it sit there for awhile, and it will start dissolving the shadow or veil of the astral plane. Then distribute it to your mental body, your emotional body and your physical body. Realize as you do so, that this process illuminates the levels of consciousness in your personality, affecting the devas and elementals in each level, and transforms the vibrations in your energy field. You can then finish your meditation by sending this light to your environment, your family, and your friends, and expand it to the whole Earth. This can be regarded as your participation in service to the whole.

Another occult meditation, which is a great tool for the development of the intuition, is as follows:
Start with the same alignment as in the first meditation, adding to it a grounding visualization by imagining a cord starting from your coccyx area and going down deep into the earth; you could also imagine roots going down from your feet. Either of these visualizations will bring your energy field deep into the earth, and through the law of compensation, the energy will move in both directions, extending also much higher above your head. Choose a seed thought before you begin. This thought could be a word or phrase that you want to receive information on, such as fear, money, soul, sadness, or anything of importance to you at the time. Sound this word in your mind and visualize the word rising higher and higher. Sound it several times, and its vibration will start invoking a response. Then, in your mind, make the sound of "Om" three times. Om is the resonance of the soul from which you want to receive your information.

Even if you do not succeed in receiving your information from the soul for a while, this process will get you closer to your higher mind. Then wait for the thought or image that comes to you. Immediately write down what you receive. It is important to keep pen and paper close at hand when doing this work, because information from these levels—no matter how concrete it seems at the time—will dissipate in the same way a dream is forgotten. Writing will also help you gain greater understanding when you read back in its totality what you have received, as there probably will be some things you had not truly grasped when you received the information, sentence by sentence. After every interruption, you can go back to your meditation, sounding the word and the Om again in your mind, until no more information is coming to you.

For the information to have a significant effect, you need to meditate on the same word for several days, with a minimum of three repetitions, as you will receive more and more meaningful information each time that you work with it. The first time might give you information on the word itself, the second time might give you more meaningful information pertaining to you, and the third time will help you integrate the information given. You can also ask, "What do I need to know about this word? How is this affecting me?" This practice will allow you to channel information from your higher mind and eventually from your soul. You can then finish with a prayer of gratitude or with the same visualization of bringing the light, as given above.

You can also finish by sounding "The Great Invocation" given to us in the A. Bailey books:

> From the point of light within the mind of God,
> Let light stream forth into the minds of men.
> Let light descend on Earth.
>
> From the point of Love within the Heart of God,
> Let Love stream forth into the Hearts of men.
> May Christ return to Earth.
>
> From the center where the Will of God is known,
> Let purpose guide the little wills of men,
> The purpose which the Masters know and serve.

> From the center which we call the race of men
> Let the plan of love and light work out
> And may it seal the door where evil dwells.
>
> Let light and love and power restore the plan on
> Earth.

"Christ" in this context refers to the soul energy, and "men" of course refers to humanity. This prayer was given at the beginning of the last century, and some of its verbiage might appear politically incorrect for our time. In fact, Lucis Trust, the publisher of all the A. Bailey books, has changed some of the words to give this invocation a more modern feel. I personally prefer the original invocation because of the numerology of each word. I also find it efficient for calling on the light, the love, and the power of the soul. However, if some of you are uncomfortable with the original words, the new version replaces Christ with "the coming one" and men with "humanity."

To get the best result, it is advisable to meditate at the same time of day and at the same place every time. This will train your subconscious mind to align and make your preparation for meditation easier and faster. You can add a little ritual, like lighting a candle or taking a crystal in your hand, as you prepare for meditation. Through the seventh Ray of divinity now in effect, the ray of order and magic, this kind of ritual will facilitate even further the alignment of your energy field.

When you encounter difficulty focusing or when your thoughts are negative, keep going with your meditation time, but use the time to pray instead. Do not try to meditate when your mind is sending negative thoughts out, as you cannot harvest flowers if you are planting weeds. Remember, occult meditation means sending thoughts out to achieve a certain result, and the higher you go, the faster the return. Do not disturb the practice and time of meditation by not doing it, but make it a time of prayer on those days when you find it difficult to achieve alignment or to quiet your mind

The days of the full moon are particularly potent for meditation, because at that time the moon is on the other side of the earth, and the sun's energy can come to us unimpeded and more powerfully. Therefore, the full moon meditation is not about connecting with the moon but rather about allowing the more evolved energy of the sun to enter our energy field with more radiance and power. This powerful energy stimulates our soul and our higher mind, as well as the lower parts of our personality. It often disturbs the consciousness of our emotional body, and many people at the time of the full moon find themselves angrier or more reactive, less able to control their emotions. Practicing meditation at the time of the full moon will be particularly productive, allowing you to channel this energy to your soul and higher mind and transmit it safely to your personality. This more organized and directed energy will then be of great benefit to all parts of you, allowing all levels to raise higher, without the emotional disturbance mentioned above.

Meditation allows us to gain understanding. By gaining understanding, we experience acceptance and then peace. Peace, or stillness of emotions, can now reflect the love and the wisdom of the soul, eradicating all fear. It transforms lower energy forms by bringing light into darkness. The devas in our energy field are part of the angelic kingdom. They are in the arc of evolution and progress along the human kingdom, toward soul energy, until they become more and more radiant and enlightened by it. The elementals are forms belonging to the physical body of the earth and are on the arc of involution. They do not evolve by moving upward to higher levels, but rather, they lose their power over us as they are transformed by the light. Because our energy field extends many feet around our physical body, we energetically touch everything within that sphere. Therefore, the devas and elementals in our energy field connect with others of their kinds in our environment, such as those forming the water, the air, or the plants, for example. With the understanding that from the emotional level and the lower level of mind we affect all life—including the elementals of the earth—we can perceive how beneficial the peace acquired is through the practice of meditation, as it will affect life and events on the physical plane. We will communicate and share this peace with all the consciousness we touch, in the same way we presently affect them by our anger and fears.

As we constantly create through our thoughts, it is important to know how to dissolve the thought forms we have created when they are outdated or no longer contribute to our evolution, unnecessarily slowing down the rate of our vibrations.

Here are two efficient energy clearing methods that you can practice with or independently of your meditation:

Whirlpool: Imagine a whirlpool of energy like a tornado starting twenty feet above your head, encompassing your entire body and energy field, and extending out for twenty feet into the ground beneath you. Visualize the whirlpool rotating very fast around you for at least five minutes, so that all the energies that need to be cleared will be taken down into the ground to be recycled. Your unwanted mental or emotional residuals will go down deep into the earth, like all the debris that goes down through the tail of a tornado. This visualization can be done daily to clear ourselves of the negative energy we receive from other people, after our work day for example, or when exposed to difficult energies in social interactions, as well as to get rid of our own negative thoughts and feelings.

Divine Fire: Connect with your Higher Self through intent and ask to be connected with the Divine Fire. This higher vibrational energy will consume outdated thought-forms, selfishness, or lower vibrational energy in your field. Create in your mind an image of large flames or little fires scattered throughout your energy field, purifying the lower energy forms. This method of clearing should be used more sparingly, once or twice a week, so that it will not disturb your nervous system.

Chapter 9 -
Our Future

The main goal of every one of us should be to control the mounting fear that automatically rises in our emotional body from experiencing insecurity and the loss of control. These emotions are greatly diminished when we understand that as a personality, we do not have real control anyway. We might have control over our actions and intentions, but not over life events, or the life of others around us. So as we dissolve the illusion that as personalities we are in control, we place more trust in the Higher Self and the guidance of our soul, following more readily the direction they are guiding us in. After all, no matter how much we try to anticipate the future, events out of our control often come and disturb our plans. Yet this disturbance is not always negative, and sometimes we find the new direction to be better than what we could have imagined from our limited viewpoint.

With the new realization that the soul has always been the one in charge, as it is the originator of life, one grows in wisdom, develops trust that everything happens for the highest good, and reaches a newfound peace. Peace always comes from the release of resistance, which in turn results in surrendering to the source. Through this alignment, humanity evolves. The mind that was the divider now accepts the unity with the soul and transfers this new realization and understanding to the personality. From that place of unity, evil and darkness cannot exist. They do not have access or entry; the door is closed; the personality has evolved. It is difficult at times to sustain this state of being, but rest assured that once it has been felt, the light will continue its descent into the personality because eventually, the mind will cease to resist.

The time between 2012 and 2025 is very short compared to the eons of human evolution, yet it will bring much transformation and elevation of consciousness throughout the human race, and consequently from there to all kingdoms in nature. We all will gain tremendously by being incarnated at this time, no matter our level of evolution. The energy presented to us will further our growth. The year 2025 will mark the beginning of an era of peace and the restitution of harmony. We will see great efforts among nations to reach agreements to further the efforts of cohabitation and cooperation.

Even though cleavages will still exist for a long time to come, much progress will be made economically and militarily for the rapprochement and wellbeing of most countries. This will be the reflection of the growth of consciousness made by humanity because of the turmoil experienced during our present challenging times. What could appear today to be a restriction of individual freedom or wealth will be perceived as a beneficial sacrifice in order to share our privileges with a larger number of people. What is willingly given will no longer be perceived as sacrifice. Sacrifice, which today we often associate with pain or difficulty, will be seen as an expression of love, a natural way of being. Sacrifice is, in reality, an expansion of consciousness and a gain rather than a loss.

The dawn of this era is yet to come, but a glimpse of this possibility will help to keep the focus on the achievement and temper the fear of change that our personalities might otherwise experience. Progress is always accompanied by a certain amount of chaos, as progress is synonymous with change. When discoveries are made, it often takes time for people to realize their importance. For example, when the personal computer came into our lives, it took time for most people to realize its value and progressive benefit. In the beginning, we could have dwelled on the loss of the multitude of jobs that would be rendered obsolete, like the stenographer, or the perforator of the coding cards who fed the monstrous computers of the time. All those trades disappeared, and people in those professions were called to evolve, to change jobs, to undertake new training. This transition affected millions of people. Twenty years later, personal computers are so much a part of our lives that we have difficulty imagining how restricting it was without them.

What we are going to experience from 2012 to 2025 is a pretty similar revolution—only this time it will be in the realm of consciousness development. The experience will create the dissolution of old patterns and new ways of seeing, thinking, and doing. At the end of this period, all of humanity will see the benefit and will be grateful for the changes, no matter how adversely any one of us might have been affected by them individually.

We cannot stop time; we are all participants. Every leader has an essential role to play, and those leaders are put in place in order for us to follow and support them in their role. This is group karma—either karma of reward or karma of retribution. In the final analysis, we are all responsible, individually, as a group or as a nation, for all events. We will learn to accept the fact that no matter the event, any moment in time is perfect. It leads us to experience exactly what we need to experience in order to evolve and gain what we need to gain. This realization, if we can truly comprehend and accept this truth, will help us through this evolution period, allowing us to experience peace and stillness even in the midst of disturbance. As we depart from the old and embrace the new, we will realize that we are leaving behind the corruption and inefficiency of our society. A new sense of pride will stimulate the desire for truth and integrity. Integrity of character will be restored to some degree. It will take many generations to purify the thoughts and desires humanity has produced, but a lesson will be learned that will influence all of us, including the generations to come. Systems of communication will be put in place that will facilitate the circulation of information in a speedy and transparent manner. A desire for truth from the general public will overcome the manipulation that might be latent in governments and large institutions. A greater sense of morality will be established, allowing much progress in the development of real spirituality.

All these things will be in place by the year 2040, but it will take until 2100 to really see most changes in the structure of the governments in many countries. These transformations will have a beneficial influence on the life of billions of people. The greatest transformation, though, will come from the changes in the exploitation of natural resources. Discoveries will be made in the use of electricity and atomic energy that will revolutionize our modes of transportation and utility services. These developments will render every country more independent and less keen to take dominion over countries that possess natural resources. This will help establish peace on most continents. The remaining difficulties will be in the fight over more prolific lands for growing food, as changes in weather patterns will have likely weakened the food production in some parts of the world. However, with the new accepted philosophy, we will see more cooperation and sharing. Barter will play an important role in the trade exchanges at the national levels. A world peace force will be put in place, and it will have much more power than the peacekeeping initiatives of today. This will prevent any individual or nation with bad intent from invading or hurting other countries and will result in more unity and cooperation amongst nations. Everyone will understand to a greater degree that we are all in the same boat, and that we will all face the same fate if the boat is leaking. We share this Earth, and we will all suffer if we do not take care of it.

We are the pioneers of this new era, even if we might not live to see its completion in our present bodies. We are laying the groundwork during this crucial time for the benefit of our children and of our souls' future incarnations. The diversity of races and beliefs need to be appreciated, the way we appreciate the diversity of flowers and trees in nature; their beauty comes from their variety of colors and shapes. As it is in the vegetable kingdom, so it is in the animal kingdom: the variety of species makes for its richness, beauty, and balance, as each plays a part in the ecosystem. Why should it be any different in the human kingdom?

The different cultures, religious beliefs, and philosophies make the human race most interesting and rich. We only need to transform the use of our mind to more beneficial and constructive purposes. As long as humanity chooses to use its intelligence to harm, we will be bound to the karma of death. The need for continuous reincarnations is only due to our need to evolve and to transform the negative karma we generate in every incarnation. Once we purify our thoughts and create compassionate and altruistic thoughts, we free ourselves from the law of karma, including the need for repetitive incarnations. We will evolve as souls, in the freedom of the all-knowing, free from the pain and fears of the limited self, and free from the limitations of movement and vision within the physical body,

The precipitation of the love of the soul on the physical plane will not only change the life we experience in physical incarnation, it will eventually eliminate those long cycles of incarnation by elevating our consciousness to higher levels where physical bodies are not needed anymore. We will evolve as souls rather than through the experiences of a succession of personalities. Repeated incarnations are part of the divine plan and purpose. Through pain and difficulty and the working out of karma, we grow in consciousness; eventually, we open our heart; when pain or fear are too great, we call on God and finally become aware of the soul—our divine origin. The cycle of incarnation stops once we are integrated with our soul, and the soul guides our personality in everything we do and think. Then there is nothing else to learn from the world of forms; all desires initiated by our emotional body will be for love and service to others. We can return to Source and continue our service from there. Every achievement of any individual transforms the body of God we are part of and help in its evolution. We are major participants in this evolution and as we cannot separate the gold from the ring; we cannot separate humanity from God's body. The more we come to this realization, the faster the progress will be.

Chapter 10 -

The Consciousness of Humanity

In our everyday life, in all our activities, and before reacting (often too fast) to what is coming our way, we should repeatedly ask ourselves, "Do I want to create conflict or harmony?" The evolution of the mind toward higher consciousness will eventually guide us toward harmony, but in this great period of transformation, conflicts will arise to force us to choose between these two opposing energies. Many will choose harmony through self-indulgence for the selfish purpose of their own tranquility, while some will be motivated by compassion for all of humanity; others will not be able to quiet their fear or their anger and will fuel conflicts. Many will choose to compromise for the sake of others, and some will choose real love from the heart as guidance rather than follow emotional drives and impulses. The numbers are important in every category, as they will determine the outcome. Will we choose to elevate our spirit, or will we choose materialism? Will we choose to experience the quality of the heart, or will we rely on material things to bring us happiness? Will we take the opportunity to lift up our consciousness, or will we prevent it from expanding? We will be called to choose. In times of transformation, no one can remain on the fence; everyone will need to choose what their individual level of participation will be.

The consciousness of the planetary Being who activates life on this planet is transforming. This transformation has a direct effect on planetary events, such as earthquakes, volcanic activity, and a change in the axis angle of the earth's poles. Therefore, even though we as humans are responsible for some of these changes, an even greater share of the responsibility lies in the transformation and the evolution of the planet itself. Many people are experiencing "resonant responses" in their bodies when the energy from an earthquake or volcanic eruption moves through the earth's lei lines. There can be a corresponding movement in our own meridian system. Some individuals are more sensitive to it than others, so the effects can be felt differently from one person to another. Sensitive people can respond to Earth changes thousands of miles from the actual event itself. Some people experience headaches or body pain when an earthquake is happening somewhere. A client called me at Christmastime, right before the tsunami occurrence in Indonesia, because he was experiencing severe panic attacks and did not know why or what to do about it. The awareness of imminent danger already happening in the astral plane is transferred from that level to the physical, via the emotional body. But even those who are less sensitive can often feel the effects.

The energy received from the sun and other planets in our solar system influences the course of development and progression of life for all consciousness in this solar system. We as human beings are responding to this flux of energy without realizing consciously where it comes from most of the time, yet we might experience periods of low energy, fatigue, and even exhaustion coupled with the inability to replenish through restful sleep. If these symptoms are not caused by strenuous activity or health problems, chances are they are due to the flux in our energy field.

All other forms of consciousness upon the earth respond to these energy fluxes as well. We have heard about astrology and the influence of the planets on our personality according to our birth sign; this is only the tip of the iceberg. Our modern astrology, reflecting humanity's lack of awareness of the soul, is really in its infancy. However, when astrology develops as a real science, we will have a greater understanding of the effect of these impulses of energy throughout our life. We will then be able to use this knowledge and understanding to make decisions according to energy patterns, and we will prepare ourselves for the changes they bring and those that we experience periodically throughout our life, rather than resisting them. Today, astrology seems relevant when viewed strictly from the angle of the personality, but often the information seems superficial or even irrelevant when one is no longer solely guided by its lower mind and emotions. In fact, the more we connect with our soul, the less our sun chart seems to make sense. In the future, astrology will tell us much more than whether it is a good time to do things, it will give us a clue as to where we are in our own evolution and will provide us with tools to more actively pursue our progression. It will reveal the karmas we are working on in any incarnation and the different Rays affecting our energy so that we can work with these concepts.

We are all interdependent on a much greater scale than we realize. The energy web that links all human beings is also the web that links the earth to other planets in our solar system, and this also links our solar system to other solar systems. Just as the organs in our body are linked to each other through blood vessels and webs of nerves, our planet is linked to other planets through energetic pathways along which light and other electric impulses travel. Life is present in every atom inside and outside our body; it pulsates on all levels of consciousness, and we are responding to it at all times. Our role is to purify and transform the energy we live in, therefore participating in the evolution of the planet. If all consciousness upon the earth had reached enlightenment previously, we would have evolved as souls, not as physical beings. As we are in a physical body, which is spirit in its densest form, our role is to bring the light into the physical level to elevate all consciousness into a much higher level of vibration, in order to transform darkness.

Some of us are trapped in this darkness, as if our feet were stuck in tar that restricts our movements and progress. Some are engulfed in what seems to be quicksand, and without help, they will not be able to extricate themselves from the prison of their own emotions. We need to help lift these people up, not abandon them. It is important for us to keep in mind that our circumstances and karma have placed every one of us into particular life experiences in order to teach us and help us progress. The goal in any lifetime is to clarify, purify, and enlighten a little bit more those consciousnesses that make up our personality—our emotional, mental, and physical bodies. The progress is slow and difficult at times. However, that which is gained is gained forever, and a time will come when the energy density around the earth will be lighter, when the illumination of the mind will bring peace and clarity to our emotions. Reflect on where we were a thousand years ago—in a barbaric and illiterate world, where fear about physical survival was the predominant preoccupation for everyone—and realize the progress we have made. Even though this struggle still exists in large parts of the world, many of us have evolved beyond harsh, extreme living conditions, and have been able to reincarnate in safer places, we call the developed countries. This is not enough, of course, for we need to continue our progression by extracting ourselves from the selfishness we most likely have fallen into in the developed world.

Materialism is another trap for most of us; it is so easy to find pleasure in the beautiful things we surround ourselves with, or to ease our insecurity or our fear of survival by accumulating wealth. We do not need to be poor or destitute to be spiritual, but balance is always the key. How much do we need to feel safe? If safety only comes to us through material accumulation, it will never be enough, as we might fear losing what we have. Only the soul can protect us and guide us into places of safety along the way. Money will not protect anyone from accident or sickness, or from the loss of a loved one. In any lifetime, everyone experiences pain as needed for our progression and for the opening of our heart. So unless we find joy and fulfillment through the help and love of one another, which indicates soul qualities, we will not find consistent joy or peace along our life journey. It will always be tainted by fear and insecurity or isolation. Only our soul can give us a sense of safety. When we receive signs of guidance and direction and we trust them, life can change drastically.

I remember a student who took my Reiki classes. She was a nurse who was very unhappy in her work and wanted to become a healer, but she could not get herself to make the leap of faith and quit her nursing job. Many emotionally excruciating weeks followed until she resolved her dilemma. One Saturday, she asked for signs of guidance to help her make the necessary choices. Lying on her lawn chair in the back yard, she fell asleep during meditation. As soon as she awoke, she noticed that the clouds above had taken the form of Reiki symbols. Immediately after, someone rang the doorbell—it was the delivery of her healing table that had been scheduled to arrive two weeks later. When she called me, she was very excited. Now able to trust her intuition, she quit her job the following Monday and moved forward with her dream.

As time progresses, we will witness many changes and transformations. For some of us, our way of living may be altered or even shattered, depending on where we live. Realize that we are taking part in a great transformation and purification of the earth itself, that our reactions to those events will affect the consciousness we live in, creating a gift or a burden for the generations to come. All consciousness must eventually be transmuted into light; this is the path of evolution. The more fear and anger we project, the denser and darker the energy our children will be born into. Only light can dissolve darkness—not war, fear, or protest. So let's focus on the light and dissolve the fears.

The earthquakes and volcanic eruptions that bring so much disruption at this time represent transformation. Some Earth changes are of our own making and can be avoided, but others are beneficial for the evolution of all consciousness. We participate in the manifestation of earthquakes, for example, by exploding bombs that create a resonance within the earth and destabilizes its integrity. Yet as the earth evolves and transforms, so does all life upon it, including the minerals composing the earth's physical body. These transformations cause Earth changes as well. The cycles might be destructive at times, but they are always to be followed by another round of evolution.

The earth, as everything in nature, follows cycles of life. The seasons in nature are similar to the cycles of human development and the cycles of every planet. The lengths of the cycles are different, but the patterns are the same. Our life experience and purpose is to help the body of the earth purify itself from gross or non-evolved matter. We do this through our thought processes, transferring to a higher vibration any non-evolved thought-form such as judgment or criticism, until eventually all consciousness will radiate light and love. This process will go on until all thoughts in the universal consciousness are cleared and enlightened and all emotion is compassionate and loving. How do we do it? Again, day by day, we invoke the help of our Higher Self to dissolve our negative thoughts and fears; we regularly clear our energy field; we dedicate ourselves to helping others. We watch our thoughts and speech and redirect all that does not express the essence of love.

We will then have contributed to the purification and elevation of consciousness of the body of the earth in which we live. We are the clearing house for the energy of the earth; we do this work through the use of our mind by bringing the light of the soul into our own individual energy field, thereby dispelling the glamour and illusions that distort the truth and keep us trapped in the physical lower experience we call life.

In this lower experience, we are lost in fears, in the illusion of separation from our own divinity and power, overtaken by the fear of abandonment, unworthiness, and isolation. We need to dispel this glamour to reconnect with truth, and to understand that we are loved. We live in the substance of the body of the one we call God in the same way that every cell of our body lives and participates in the consciousness we call a human being. There is no separation, just a maze of energy that holds us all together in which we affect positively or negatively, depending on the thoughts and emotions we send into it. The path of evolution is to bring the light into the energy web so that shadows can be dispelled and the truth of the higher consciousness can touch our minds. This is the path of return to the soul for every life—to be free from the claws of the lower consciousness that keeps us trapped in cycles of incarnation.

These are inevitable cycles; we need to experience them, as they are the way to receive the lessons needed to enrich the soul and reach a higher knowledge. However, the length of these cycles depends upon us and our ability and determination to bring in this higher consciousness that will eventually free us individually, and finally free all of humanity from the endless cycle of negative karma that we continue to generate. The way to stop the cycle of negative karma is to practice harmlessness in thought, action, and speech. Most religions enjoin its followers to "do no harm," and many professions, such as medicine or psychology include the injunction "do no harm" in their code of ethics, it is part of the Hippocratic Oath. The importance of harmlessness cannot be understated. Yet for all we have been told, how far have we come in the practice of harmlessness? A quick glance at the headlines and at our own actions at the end of the day will sadly tell us that we can do better.

How, then, can we put harmlessness into practice? Like many other aspects of self-improvement, awareness is the key. One practical tool we can all use is the "daily review." At the end of each day, we take a fifteen-minute review of our day: our experiences, thought projections, speech content, and interactions with others. We can ask ourselves, "Did I practice harmlessness in all of those categories today, or did I succumb to angry, competitive, and unloving words and thoughts?" We must purify, clarify, and bring the light to these moments, and learn through awareness how to redirect our thoughts and energy projection. Moreover, we must learn how to extract ourselves from gossipy situations and keep our thoughts pure. The reward will be profound; our hearts will open. The light of the soul will radiate upon us, and we will be released from the entrapment of the many fears in our lower personality. In order for us to participate in the healing of the earth, we must clear the energy of our thoughts and emotions. Not only will we elevate the consciousness of humanity, the earth will actually cleanse itself from the pollution of its air and water. If we care for the earth and want to save it, remember that our negative thoughts and emotions are the most polluting agents, as they are affecting the elemental and devic consciousness of the water and the air.

Dr. Masaru Emoto shows us in his book *Messages from Water,* the incredible differences in the water molecules that occur in correspondence to the emotions or images projected upon them. He came to the conclusion that the water in his experiments reacted to the actual words that carry the emotional energy, no matter the language.

Another example comes from an experiment using two beaker jars, each with a cotton ball inside. One jar was focused upon with loving thoughts, and the word "angry" was written on the other. The "angry" jar grew moldy while the "loving thoughts" jar remained mold free.

This period of transformation is a unique opportunity for all lives upon the earth, as we will benefit from a much higher energy coming to us from the cosmos. It calls for movement and transformation and is the dawn of a new higher and richer grade of experience for all kingdoms in nature. The time to experience peace and regard for all life comes as we seek to evolve. As we progress, we transcend fear and cease resisting the present transformations. As unpleasant and even as scary as they may seem at times, they are bringing the ideals of love, peace, tolerance, compassion, and understanding into physical reality. We are co-creators of our experiences. Bring love when others might bring hatred, bring understanding when others might be inflexible and righteous, and bring compassion when others bring intolerance. This will not only transform those of us who choose to bring the light, it will eventually transform others as well and ultimately transform the world.

When we are surrounded by negative people, we must influence them, instead of allowing them to influence us. This is not always an easy thing to do, so we should avoid self-condemnation when we sometimes fail. Instead, we simply try again. At first we may be able to remain in the light just 10 percent of the time. With practice and patience, our loving thoughts will increase until they are part of us. We will embody this consciousness; our personality will have become the expression of the soul. You are light, you are love, and you have the power to transform the energy and the lives around you. It is hard work, but how long do we want to live in pain? This work is surely worth trying, especially when the alternative is the pattern of pain.

As humanity starts to perceive truth, the lower consciousness will be greatly altered. Ideas of cooperation, understanding, and unity will permeate the mind. Many will have the desire to create sustainable communities. Some will simply get more connected to others in their neighborhood, helping one another more. The distortion presently created by our lower mind's interpretation and misperception of reality is the source of various kinds of illusion.

In the new era, many highly evolved old souls, or "white magicians," will reincarnate for the purpose of transmuting the lower energy of thought forms and emotions, which were created in Atlantean days, into the light. Because of the Seventh Ray influence, many souls will incarnate to work with this energy. Some of these old souls will work for the greater good, using the energy of the soul to create for the highest good of all; they will be the white magicians. Unfortunately, others will still continue to work for selfish purposes from their lower personality, creating solely for their own benefit; they are known as the "black magicians."

Much information will circulate about manifesting; this information has already begun to appear. In order to stay in the light, discrimination and discernment will be necessary for everyone to determine what sounds true and resonates with them individually. Both darkness and light will be present, and in fact, both need to be present in order for us to learn to recognize the difference and eventually choose between these two presentations of truth. Both black and white magicians have power. The black magician is motivated to use his power for selfish purposes and the satisfaction of the personality—using the elementals, the non-evolved consciousness of the earth—to create, while the white magician uses his power for the highest good of all, creating under the supervision and with the substance of soul consciousness. The white magicians trust in the soul to give to the personality all that it needs to do the work and free it from physical concerns. The personality, therefore, releases all concern and fear to attend to the need of the hour. When one is connected with Source, working from the heart in any chosen field, or dedicated to the work of helping others, all is given to the personality to allow one to do that work. When people want power over others, as well as material satisfactions, they use black magic to the detriment of their own soul's evolution.

Again, we are composed of living consciousnesses; the atoms in our physical and energetic bodies form our "subconscious selves." They evolve in accordance with the quality of our thoughts and emotions. When we bring the light to these consciousnesses, we promote their evolution and growth within that light. This is a great service to them and to the whole; the soul evolves greatly by such activity and achievement. To the contrary, when we use these consciousnesses to service only our personality, we keep them in darkness, in the non-evolved substance of the lower energy levels. There is no advancement for any of these consciousnesses in that particular lifetime. The soul loses a lot from activity limited to the lower personality levels, delaying its evolution, not only because there is no progression in that lifetime, but because the personality is more entrapped in the non-evolved levels and has more karmas to overcome in future incarnations. For this reason, anyone using their mental ability to intentionally manifest their physical reality should really take these facts into consideration, closely examining their motivation and realizing the consequences of their intention.

These days, much emphasis is given to the power of the mind and its ability to manifest. However, there is usually no good explanation of the mechanism and consequence of these kind of activities on the subconscious self and on the soul. Usually, only the personality desires and its need for instant gratification are taken into consideration. People following the various teachings of manifestation are in great danger of succumbing to the activity of black magic, creating more negative karmas for themselves and for humanity as a whole.

I would, therefore, highly recommend that any activity of conscious manifestation be taken under soul guidance and surrendered to soul intention. Put the needs of the personality aside, unless those needs also carry an altruistic intent, or a higher purpose to help others, whether human, animal, plant, or the earth itself. Remember, when one is occupied servicing the needs of others, his or her own needs are taken care of. This is called "being in the flow of the source," or "give and you shall receive." Even in the most evolved personalities, many of the desires we want to manifest carry both selfish and altruistic intents. We are human, so this is inevitable. However, using our knowledge to manifest money or a fancy new car for our personal satisfaction creates a lot of disruption in our advancement. Yet if we manifest a much-needed car to help transport goods to elderly people who cannot attend to their own needs, we then create good karma. Everything depends on the purity of our intention.

The events leading up to and around 2012 are for the purpose of redirecting our thoughts and emotions and the consciousness of humanity from lower to higher vibrations. The lessons are harder if we resist; therefore, the more we focus on the purpose of any event, the less difficult the lessons will be. If we can trust that change is happening for the highest good of all, we will need fewer drastic learning tools, such as destruction and discomfort. This truth has been given before to humanity in other civilizations, and for the most part, it has been ignored. Yet the evolution is constant, and even though power has been given equally to the light and to the darkness, humanity today is more apt to balance the scale toward the light because of the larger number of truly conscious and thoughtful individuals. The cooperation of the Hierarchy of Souls, at this particular time, is directed toward helping in the rediscovery of old truths—among other things—through the resurfacing of old manuscripts and artifacts, as well as bringing new understanding and identification to the ones already discovered, thus further promoting the advancement of science and discoveries such as DNA and carbon dating. These discoveries will lead to the dissolving of illusions created through the ages, especially in the realm of religion.

An example of this comes from Egyptian farmer Muhammad Ali, who in 1945 was collecting lime from the hillside at Nag Hammadi and stumbled upon a buried earthen tube containing the Mary Magdalene "Gnostic Gospels." Other artifacts will be discovered, as we progress, which will shed light on some of man's evolution.

In the past century, much emphasis has been given to the development of science and industrialization. This emphasis was due to the activity of the Fifth Ray of Concrete Knowledge and Science, present upon the earth from 1775 until a few decades ago. This emphasis has produced the necessary impulse within the minds of modern scientists, leading to considerable technological progress. However, there is now a need to integrate the progress made thus far, ensuring that it will be used responsibly before any more is given so fast and on such a large scale. Again, we have the light and the darkness working side-by-side. The wonder and power of the atom as a source of electricity has been used for the benefit of mankind. Unfortunately, it has also been used for evil and destructive purposes. Because of the leap in the development of the mind, and the corresponding lag in the opening of the heart, the Fifth Ray has been temporarily withdrawn from the earth, though not from individual people. Science will still progress, but more slowly. Consciousness needs to develop along with the revelations of science for our own safety.

Chapter 11 -
Earth Changes

The first consideration in these challenging times is the safety of human lives. As always, people have a choice in their experience, deciding where they want to live and how open they want to be to their inner guidance. The next fifty years will see transformation in the topography of some countries. Some lands will need to be purified. Water and fire are the natural means of purification for the earth. As a measure of precaution and for safety, the coasts, in general, need to be avoided—and they will not be the only source of transformation. Other interferences will come in the form of floods, volcanic eruptions, and fires. Some states in the United States are more vulnerable than others, but the most devastating possibilities are an earthquake of great magnitude in California, with ramifications in Washington State, and the eruption of the Yellowstone volcano.

At this time, the more advanced beings of the planet, both in and out of incarnation, along with the Anteriens, are working to minimize the earth movements. These events, of course, would be devastating for millions of people directly in the vicinity of the aforementioned areas, but also for the whole United States, as well as other countries, significantly disrupting the food supply and the weather patterns in most states and around the globe. This can be avoided as more people awaken their consciousness and participate in the precipitation of love and light in the physical plane, affecting positively the devas and elementals forming the earth elements.

Direct guidance is necessary for each one of us individually to know where it is safe to live, as other minor events will continue to disturb the earth's energy in order to create movements that will push us in our evolution. However, because our thoughts create our reality, do not seek guidance from a position of fear but rather from a loving openness. Realize that there is a benefit for the soul even in catastrophes where thousands of people are killed or displaced, as it elicits a great wave of compassion from a large part of humanity all over the world, helping to further the development of altruism. It would be more desirable, though, for people to start developing compassion out of their own accord, without the need for it to be brought out through suffering.

Other countries will suffer from earthquakes as well. We have to realize that the bombs of warfare exploding around the world are not just affecting the local terrain of war-torn regions; they have a direct effect on the earth globally. The earth responds to the trembling of the ground. Sound waves emitted by exploding bombs create holes in the etheric or energetic body of the earth. People must awaken to the effects human actions and behaviors have on the earth itself. Again, we are, in large part, the creators of our life circumstances.

The most difficult event we may face will be the pollution of the water supply and the subsequent scarcity of clean drinking water. The help given by higher evolved beings is not enough to avoid all these problems. We need to start taking responsibility, individually and as communities, to change our habits and purify our behaviors and our thoughts. We pollute as much through emotions and the thoughts we project as our lack of care for the environment pollutes the air and the ground we live upon.

When considering the problems facing humanity today, we should take action. First, we should raise our consciousness to produce loving, positive thoughts, rather than adding to the problem by projecting anger or fear. Second, we should act with more awareness. Practicing this regularly will raise our vibrations and connect us closer to the guidance from the Higher Self. In doing so, we will not only help ourselves, we will participate in the healing of all humanity.

As time passes, it will become apparent that transformation does not only have physical implications but that it also touches the emotional and mental structures of humanity. Inflexibility among religious leaders who want to control others will no longer resonate with the general public—at least not with the current intensity. The fanatics in any religion will become fewer in number. This will be due to the events that will open the minds of many and to the diminishing intensity of the Sixth Ray of Devotion and Idealism. People who are so sure they possess the truth will be challenged and pushed to reevaluate their beliefs. This process will result in difficult periods of emotional insecurity for some people, yet subsequently, it will lead them to the perception of a greater truth.

The storm is always followed by a period of rest and clarity. The light that will follow the storm will illuminate many minds. As it radiates out into the world, its influence will heal and transform many lives for the better. This illumination will dissipate darkness on much deeper levels than at any previous time and will establish a suitable energy channel for the most advanced souls who will then be able to incarnate. The beings who exist on the spiritual side of the veil have long prepared for the dawn of this New Age. As we evolve by dissolving the shadow in our lower selves, we will be able to accommodate and sustain the vibration of a higher, more-evolved consciousness.

Chapter 12 –
Intuition Development

All happenings result in positive and negative effects. There will be a positive side to the earth cataclysms, whether through water or fire, as they will clear some of the density of the astral plane, thus allowing freer entrance to the light of the soul in the physical realm. This will facilitate the expansion of the tremendous lateral development in communication that we have achieved, taking it to a vertical dimension as well. Consequently, this web of multidimensional communication will be used to foster unity between countries and individuals, as well as to promote group work. The number of people working in groups multiplies and amplifies the power of the energy of the soul to bring the desired results more rapidly and more powerfully. It will also help in the development of our minds, awakening our faculty of thought via the stimulation of the information flow presented. The more knowledge we receive, the more educated decisions everyone can make.

Yet here again we find the need to develop discrimination and discernment to avoid being tricked by the false or manipulative information that will be generated by individuals responding to the force of darkness. Ultimately, every one of us needs to develop our intuition, even if it happens through trial and error, so that we can eventually recognize the vibration of truth in all our activities.

Real intuition comes from the soul. Many people mistake intuition with instinct. Instinct comes from the solar plexus, the seat of the lower mind. It is the animal instinct, one that links a mother to her child or warns us of danger. It is also the place of lower telepathic communication that allows us to read other people's energy. We can receive insights from the solar plexus; however, this is not intuition. The development of intuition involves learning to connect with our soul in order to receive information from outside the personality. From the soul we have access to the past and to the future. We can gather higher knowledge and receive communication from members of the Hierarchy as they always solely communicate through our soul. Once we are able to make contact with our own soul, we can then have contact with higher beings or members of the Hierarchy. Higher beings will not communicate with our personality, because no purpose is served in giving information to someone who has not developed spiritual consciousness, and because their higher energy vibrations would fry our nervous system, so to speak. Until we have reached the soul, our energy field will not have been elevated to the vibrational level needed for contact with higher beings.

Developing our intuition requires raising our vibrations through purity of life, intent, and speech. The process is aided through the practice of occult meditation, as we consciously clear our energy fields and practice channeling information, like in the seed thought meditation given earlier.

Because we can receive information from different parts of ourselves, it can be confusing and difficult, especially at first, to discern the source of the information we are receiving. So here are few helpful insights about real guidance:

Genuine guidance will not flatter you or tell you how wonderful or needed you are. Genuine guidance will never boss you around or tell you forcefully that you have to do something. True guidance gives suggestions and the choice is always yours. Genuine guidance will not give you information that will scare you. For example, instead of telling you that you will be at risk for having an accident today, it will encourage you to take another road instead. Genuine guidance will never push you to fight or to get even. The soul is the embodiment of love and wisdom; there is always a more compassionate way to achieve or to detach.

The stronger the voice of guidance received, the lower will be the vibrational level of its source. The voice of the soul or the Higher Self can be as soft as a passing thought—one that in hindsight you may wish you had heeded. Deciphering the voice of guidance is a difficult skill to master, of course, but intuition is so useful in everything we do that it is worth the effort. Any step forward in making progress is a gain in this lifetime and the starting point for our next incarnation. As an incentive, remember that we are in a time period where the light is more accessible and where a larger number of more advanced souls are coming into incarnation, raising the vibrations of many others. Therefore, the work and the achievement are greatly facilitated and energetically supported for the ones who decide to walk the path of intuition development and of transformation.

This descent of the light is partly responsible for the apparent chaos, as it creates resistance and reaction among the less advanced consciousness around the earth, including the consciousnesses in our emotional bodies. This should not drive us to stop bringing in the light; on the contrary, we should intensify our work because once the light comes with enough intensity, it will transform and help those consciousnesses to evolve as well. It will finally produce peace and cooperation among humanity and in all the kingdoms below us.

As the time approaches for this transformation, astrological alignments will bring energies that will guide, facilitate, and direct the coming changes. We will move, either harmoniously or dramatically through them, depending on the level of development we have achieved individually and as a whole, for it will dictate our ability to absorb and integrate the energies in manifestation.

The more we prepare now, the easier the transition will be later. Negative karma can be altered and transformed by good deeds. Though the period we are now living in is called the Dark Age, it can be illuminated and transformed by the elevation in consciousness of humanity, thus preventing the law of retribution from forcing us into calamity and disaster. At its root, our solar system is under Ray 2, the Ray of Love and Wisdom, and all that is evolving in it is expressing those qualities. Every consciousness in this solar system will evolve through the expression of this Ray of Love. The essence of the One in whom we live, whom we call God, is love, and that essence is forgiving, compassionate, and not resentful or hateful as some religions would have us believe. Every effort to express this love and compassion by anyone is acknowledged and recognized by the soul and contributes to its evolution.

Eventually, the love, acceptance, and compassion for all parts of ourselves are the key to healing for every one of us. When we can heal ourselves in this way, only then are we able to reflect this acceptance and compassion toward others, as all we give and experience is always a reflection of ourselves emotionally and mentally. We are our most severe judge and juror: we constantly criticize and condemn our thoughts, actions, weaknesses, and failures.

This lack of acceptance and compassion toward ourselves creates great disruption and bitterness in our emotional body, as well as inflexibility and distress in our mental body. As energy travels downward, our physical body expresses these negative energies through illness, either physical or mental, as the brain is part of the physical body. Love needs to be applied to ourselves first. This is possible when the love of the soul is felt and applied, and the light does its healing work. This healing work is a necessary step to raise our vibrations and develop our intuition.

Here is an exercise you can use to help your mind shift from judgment to appreciation of yourself and to give encouragement to all consciousnesses in the different levels of your energy field:

- Sit quietly, close your eyes, and take a deep breath to relax your body.
- Imagine the radiant light of the soul above your head, and bring it down to your crown chakra and then to your throat and heart.
- This light is also love, so allow yourself to feel the love in your heart. Then through intent send it to your lower mental body. Give gratitude to your mind for its intelligence, its ability to help you in your daily life by helping you take care of all things in your work or in your home. Give your mind gratitude for its creativity and for its ability to imagine and explore.
- Bring this love to your emotional body, and give gratitude to this part of yourself for its ability to feel the warmth of another's touch, and to allow you to vibrate with appreciation to music, dancing, or the visual arts. Give gratitude to your emotional body for allowing you to appreciate beauty in your life and to connect lovingly with others.
- Finally, bring this love to your physical body and give it gratitude for allowing you to move, walk, dance, hug. Give gratitude to your physical body for allowing you to be alive.

As you do this exercise, you will realize that all parts of you are good, even if they are not all attuned to the light yet. Giving appreciation to those parts that compose your personality will help you realize that they also need understanding and compassion. From compassion will come forgiveness; it is well known that only when you forgive yourself can you truly forgive others.

Chapter 13 -
Manifestation

The planetary transformation we are now witnessing can be affected and altered by the consciousness of humanity in the same way our physical health is affected by the thoughts in our mental body and the emotions in our emotional body. We as humanity live in the energy field of the earth. Consequently, our emotional and mental states affect the energy field of the earth, which in turn affects the physical body of the earth. In this transformation, we can create greater harmony—or greater chaos. Both will affect all living creatures and consciousness on and around the earth, from the densest form, the mineral kingdom, to the consciousness of the souls in the higher spectrum of evolution.

Due to the development of our mental capabilities, humanity has acquired the ability to participate consciously in the transformation and evolution of the earth. The cycles of life and evolution will be respected, but within these cycles much latitude is given to us to co-create and transform our world. This is done by the use of our creative imagination and our power to manifest through our thoughts and desires. Whatever we choose to empower, we will create in our reality. Some of us find it hard to believe it is just that simple and that we can really change our world and our experiences, but it is so. The difficulty to achieve results comes from the fact that it is often difficult to control our thoughts. We project thoughts of true desires and intentions mixed with thoughts of fear or incredulity. This is why it is important to progress in our ability to focus our mind, undisturbed by unwanted emotions and clear in our intent. For manifestation to happen, we need to energize the thought-form we created, empowering it continuously with desire until it manifests. The further we progress in the development of our consciousness, the more in touch we become with the divine energy we are part of, and the more help we receive from the spiritual world. Then we realize and understand the possibilities in front of us.

However, the downfall these possibilities bring is that darkness will also rise and escalate as light progresses. This will come from the use of this knowledge by individuals reaching for personal power and control over others. Every individual soul is divine, as it is the evolved part of God's consciousness. Consequently, anyone trying to dominate and enslave another being is, in fact, through the law of karma, enchaining himself to that soul. This includes trying to attract a particular person romantically or manipulating someone to do something we want him to do using manifestation techniques. Anyone who tries to control or dominate other individuals will experience being controlled and dominated as a way to learn and evolve. Anyone who uses mind control in order to direct others for his own benefit will lose the power of his mind in the present or the following incarnation, until he has opened his heart sufficiently to use his power safely for himself and others.

Noted psychic Edgar Cayce said that whatever good is given to us, in any particular incarnation, will be removed from us in subsequent lives if we mishandle or do not appreciate it, until we learn to feel gratitude for or appreciate what we have been given. So do not take for granted your good looks, your health, or your abundance; appreciate it, feel gratitude for it, and use gracefully and compassionately what you have been blessed with, especially with others less fortunate. This is the way toward growth and evolution. It will allow you to add more blessings to what you already have in your next incarnation, rather than lose what you had previously gained.

In the centuries to come, most of this teaching will be common knowledge. This will lead people to use more responsibly what they have—gifts from nature. Gifts are earned in the same way hardships are earned. We do not experience anything we have not created in this life or in previous ones or that we have not opened our mind to and put into motion. Our thoughts are the mighty creators of our reality, and we empower everything and anything that we allow our minds to entertain. This is worth repeating, for if you cannot control your fears or if you thrive on the possibility of catastrophes, upheaval, and war, you are empowering those possibilities and participating in their physical manifestation. Some people will gain monetarily or ideologically from these events. They want them to happen and they empower these energies with their thoughts and desires.

But you who are reading this book can exercise other choices. Do not fall into the frenzy created in the universal consciousness by the kind of people who would choose chaos. Leave your emotion behind and rise to the level of your mind: what do you want to see happening? Do you want transformation and evolution to happen through chaos, or do you want it to happen with harmony? Do you want millions of people to die or to suffer due to destitution and fear, or do you want their minds to be illuminated progressively by the higher consciousness of their soul? What do you want to experience yourself?

Reality will be experienced through pain or through peace. Do not believe it will happen to others and not to you. This is group karma, for humanity is a whole; we will all be affected by the events, whether economic upheaval or physical destruction. So what do you want to empower, and what do you want to help create? The future can be affected and transformed through our thought processes and the focus of our mind and intentions. So visualize harmonious world relationships and compassionate actions taking place; project joyful thoughts animated by loving desires into your life and the lives of others. This will counteract the fearful and destructive projection of energy presently fermenting in the universal consciousness. The choice is ours and as always, I choose to believe that you will join me in empowering the light.

In order to participate in this transformation, you can use this manifestation technique as often as you want to: Visualize the earth surrounded by golden light, and ask for this light to touch the heart and minds of all humanity, especially of all world leaders, in all departments, and in public affairs, so they can lead humanity in accordance with the work of the Hierarchy of light.

Chapter 14 -
The Appearance of the New Race

The building of a new society based on the recognition of spiritual truths and the development of a human race with higher values rests far beyond 2025. However, the development of consciousness during the next fifteen years will be such that we can expect some dissolution of the illusions and of the distortions in which we are presently subjected. This will result in a greater perception of truth and, consequently, a higher degree of discernment for most people.

The movement toward this awareness began with the generations who came after WWII. They brought into reality for the first time the notion of unity and love amongst people. They expressed love in the 1960s in their peaceful rebellion against war; we called them "flower children." These people have grown and acquired maturity. They continue to express this impetus of love through many foundations and charities, in ways and in numbers we have never seen before in the history of humanity. Many organizations are dedicated to helping all lives, from the preservation of lands and forests, to the welfare of animals and humans. Many realize their role is to help the ones who cannot help themselves.

This trend will continue, as the souls coming into incarnation are more and more advanced. To allow their descent, the vibrations need to be of a more refined quality. Many from earlier generations have achieved sufficient development to positively affect the energy around the earth and allow the physical incarnation of the more advanced souls. As the souls incarnating are more and more evolved, they become a source of disruption as much as a blessing, because it is a law of the universe that the light disturbs the darkness before it dissolves it. These newly evolved souls produce personalities with higher vibrations and enhanced sensitivity. This creates friction and resistance with the more dense and established energies in our society. Discomfort is experienced on both sides.

The new generations are misunderstood and are being asked to adapt to environments and school systems that are outdated and do not take their intelligence and their sensitivity into consideration. These old souls are coming in physical incarnation to reform our present civilization. They are labeled "ADD" or "unruly." They are misunderstood, at the least. School systems and psychologists promote the use of drugs to help these children focus or be more disciplined in the classroom, instead of looking at the real problem. These children are bored, are under—and over—stimulated, and are unable to adapt to the school environment while their needs are not being met by our present educational system.

As many people have come to realize, these kids are not dysfunctional but are extremely sensitive. They are, in fact, the most advanced members of the human race. Their sensitivity makes them receptive to the energy of everyone around them. This brings distress and often great pain to these young personalities, whose immature brain prevents them from understanding and filtering the information they receive. Because of this, they often develop low self-esteem as they recognize they are not quite like their peers, and often do not get the grades they try to achieve; they do not fit into the system. They often become rebellious, as they also know, subconsciously, that they are here to reform the institutions. On the other hand, the denser personalities who are part of the status quo feel frustrated having to deal with these children; they do not know how to handle or to teach them.

Our system of education needs to change. Even though we recognize more and more our children's intelligence, we fail to substantially change our methods of teaching, preferring to medicate a large portion of the school population. Instead of adapting ourselves and our learning structures to their needs, we try to put them "in a box" they have long outgrown. As long as the energetic component of each human being is not recognized and acknowledged, we will continue to create friction on both sides. The old methods will not sustain us. We cannot continue to medicate more and more children to artificially create in them what we consider acceptable behavior. We need to realize that we are the ones who need to change and adapt to them, and we need to learn to listen to what their behaviors are communicating. They are bright. They are creative. They are sensitive. Rather than just temporarily containing them, we need to help them by teaching them tools and strategies that will help them regulate themselves.

The first tool to teach them is energy management. It will allow them to emotionally detach from their environment and protect themselves from the overload of heightened sensory perception. We also need to develop new methods of teaching that would give them more mental and creative stimulation. It is recognized that children learn better when they participate in physical activities. We need to teach through play, through interesting games, instead of lecturing them while they are sitting on a chair. They would then be interested in the subjects presented, instead of being bored in their classrooms.

Educators constantly elevate the level of difficulty in curriculum tests and exams to fit the rise of student intelligence but change our methods of teaching very little. Some children make it through while some don't. We owe it to all of them and to ourselves to help these highly sensitive children and to nurture them and help them avoid depression and self-medication with drugs and alcohol—those devastating substances sensitive teens often seek refuge with when the difficulty of adolescence overwhelms and the pressures from peers and school increase. I do not imply that all drug users or alcoholics are of this new breed of children, but these substances are too readily available now and are becoming what could appear to be an easy relief to the pain experienced by this new generation. When they face too many difficulties and put-downs, these young personalities are unable to channel their intense energy into positive outlets, in accordance with their souls' level of development.

Adapting our methods of education to this new breed of children does not equal permissiveness. To give them the stability and safety they need, they need structure and boundaries more than ever and more than others. They also need more transition time between tasks or play. They need to know in advance what the next activity is going to be so they can prepare themselves mentally for the transition. Without this preparation time, they will resist and refuse to do anything asked of them. Their first answer will always be no, no matter what it is, when they are caught off guard. So to avoid conflict, warn them at least fifteen minutes in advance what will be taking place next, so they have the time to accustom themselves to the idea. Their minds will have a transition period to prepare for the change of activity and to let go of what they are often so focused and engrossed in.

Above all, these beautiful children need a lot of love and reassurance because they often feel insecure as a result of their extreme sensitivity. We can be firm without being mean; we can listen with patience, opening our minds to avoid criticizing them. They need to feel safe in spite of their frequent inability to control themselves and their emotions. We need to realize that they hear us without words; they are telepathic, empathic, and receptive to all energies around them. As any parent of one of these children knows, hiding our feelings or thoughts from them is useless. They know. They perceive our worries, no matter how much we try to hide them, and because we often try to hide our negative states of mind from them, it creates more fear and insecurity in these children. They often think they have done something wrong, that we the parents are displeased with them. Taking the time to explain in simple words what is bothering us, using minimal details, will help them to release the fear that they might be responsible or unsafe. It is so important that we genuinely change ourselves to embrace who they are and not to force on them what we expect them to be based on our old beliefs and limitations. We have to look at them as our most precious treasure, nurture them, and allow them to be and to achieve their lifetime purpose. Unfortunately, most of us are handicapped by our fears, including our fear regarding them and by the old ways of coping that we learned from our parents.

Letting go of the old is the first teaching that they bring to us, forcing us to move through our own fears and limitations in order to help them. All the parents of such children will recognize themselves in this dynamic. They will recognize their children's various struggles, fears, and pain. To these parents, I say: stop resisting. You only make matters worse for them and for yourselves. Drop your fears for them and their future; they are protected and guided. You are just their guardian. They have been entrusted to your care for a short part of their lives; the rest is up to them and their Higher Selves. The best support you can give them is acceptance and love. Then they will grow strong roots to anchor themselves and wings to fly. The stability and self-confidence developed through love and acceptance will allow them to thrive freely toward their purpose and walk the path of their soul without the inhibition of your fears and worries. You will learn from them, grow from them, and be transformed by them.

The opening of the heart is the goal of the root race we are presently evolving toward. They are challenging us to do it, to move through our fears, our limitations, our preconceived ideas, our pride, and our intolerance. They are offering us a great gift—if only we can recognize it.

Embrace these children. Love them to the fullest of your ability. Accept them unconditionally. Help them to accept themselves in a society not quite ready for them. It is not just a gift to them, it is a gift to yourself. What you will gain will propel you to great personal development and evolution. For those of you who are parents, realize that, after all, they have chosen you as parents, which means you have the capability to understand them and to work through your frustration when they do not behave as you think they should.

Look at yourself. Did you agree with all that your parents expected of you, or did you have conflict with them as they tried to put you in a preformed mold? Often these children come to parents who themselves are more advanced, with different vibrations than the rest of the family. Did you have the feeling you did not fit in as a child, or were considered the black sheep of the family? If so, that is why your children came to you. Use your experience to understand them and steer them in the right direction, be their best ally, and use your mature judgment to help them integrate their life lessons along with the love they need.

As humanity progresses in its development, help from the Hierarchy of souls will be given to guide the race and elevate our consciousness. The children coming to us will be more and more advanced with each generation. The colors perceived by the physical eyes will change, as they will reflect the higher vibrations we will be able to access. The purification of our energy field will allow us to rise to consciousness levels that will permit us to retrieve information and truths not yet accessible. As the race advances, so will all other lives on Earth. Evolution will happen in every kingdom in nature, and the elevation will affect the earth itself. New uses for the minerals of the earth will bring that kingdom to newly elevated consciousness with a higher quality of service to humanity. Because of the spiritual development of the human race, discoveries in science will be most often used for the good or positive purposes, rather than negative ones. This will create a chain reaction that will benefit all who exist upon the earth, from the consciousness of the atom to the planetary consciousness. It is said that one particle of matter affects the whole. We can see this with the avatars who have walked the earth, such as Buddha, Jesus, and others. These avatars have individually changed the consciousness of millions of people on Earth. One single consciousness has affected us all.

As we progress, we will transform in consciousness as well as genetically. Our energetic body is the mold that cradles our physical body. What happens in the outer energetic levels, which we call the subconscious, reveals itself through our appearance and our way of being.

On an individual scale, for example, someone who becomes depressed for a long period of time will often change in their physical appearance. It is not only the change in their vibrations we may feel about them, but in a short period of time, they either gain or lose a sizeable amount of weight, depending on their individuality. Their body reflects their state of mind. One of my clients gained twenty pounds within two months of the loss of her father, yet without ever mentioning her weight in our sessions together, I helped her transform her emotional state, and she rapidly lost the excess weight.

As we evolve, the new race will be taller and thinner. Bodies will be more refined and more sensitive to perception through all the senses: smell, taste, hearing, sight, and touch. All senses will be enhanced, and a "new" sense will be added—the sense of higher perception, which we call intuition, leading eventually to telepathy. We will realize how limiting words are as we will be able to capture and transmit messages and information from one mind to another, like radio waves. Intuition is, in fact, a form of telepathy between the soul and the mind.

It is possible to contemplate how this telepathic ability will also be used in a lateral transmission between minds through the energetic grid of the earth that interconnects us all. This is already happening on a mass scale. When an idea is created and added to the universal consciousness, it is then received by the minds of many individuals. This telepathic interplay is at the root of all mass movements and ideologies, or in a more simplistic way in the following of fashion trends such as clothing and design style. As we evolve and refine our sensory systems, we will be able to consciously transmit and receive individual thoughts directed to us or emitted by us, without the need for these thoughts to be amplified. This is already happening between people who have never met, though more often between people who have a close connection to one another, like couples, or parents and children. For example, this occurs when one person thinks about something and the other person verbalizes it at the same time.

Telepathic communication will not only be developed for communication between humans, it will also be used for animal communication. This will result in a greater evolution in the animal kingdom, through the embryonic development of their minds. Connecting with the animal mentally will bring a greater awareness of our interconnection with them, their value, and their service to the earth. This will also represent the end of the negative karma linking humanity to the animal kingdom.

A. Bailey tells us that we eat the flesh of animals because in Lemurian times, animals used to hunt and kill us during our first animal-man physical root race. Once this interconnectedness is recognized and the mental connection established, all humanity will become vegetarian, regarding and caring for all animals in the way we presently do for our beloved domesticated animals. Anyone who relates emotionally and mentally with his pets would never think of eating them; this same impulse will someday describe the attitude of all of humanity toward the entire animal kingdom. This coming change in nutrition is one of the components that will eventually change the genetics of human bodies. There is truth to the old saying, "You are what you eat."

Today's largely meat-based diet has two interesting effects on human beings. First, meat is grounding. Without the grounding property of the meat, people will be more able to easily raise their vibrations. Second, when we eat meat, we actually ingest fear. Animals experience fear at the time of death, and that fear-energy remains in the imprint of their cells. When we consume these cells, we bring that energy into our own body, which in turn leaves its signature on our cells. As every cell in our physical body has corresponding atoms in our emotional field, the emotional bodies of people will thus be helped to be more settled when, in due time, vegetarianism is established among all of humanity.

The change in diet is a drive that will come gradually, as our taste for food changes as our energy changes. It is not to be forced on anyone. On the other hand, some of the Indigo children confound their parents by refusing to eat meat. It is important for parents to be sensitive to their children's needs or values and to balance the vegetarian impulse with sound nutritional guidance, rather than forcing them to eat meat, as this would not be in harmony with their vibrations. Parents can take heart in knowing that entire cultures thrive on vegetarian diets and still provide their children with many healthy choices.

Telepathic communication will also happen with the other kingdoms in nature, such as trees and plants, as we will learn to respect all life, realizing that there is nothing in existence that is not part of the body of God. We will respect and value all life forms.

Telepathic communication will force us to monitor our thoughts with greater care. This awareness will guide us to make deliberate choices toward more positive thinking. This change in the nature of our thoughts will be responsible for the transformation of the creation we participate in collectively. Our reality will be transformed as we transform our thoughts. Anyone who has already chosen to change his way of thinking knows his life has changed as a result, reverberating what he has consciously decided to pay attention to and to project on others.

I have experienced this in my own life. I see it in the lives of my clients when they report that people around them have changed and that others treat them differently, when in fact, their surroundings are only responding to and reflecting their new energy projection. Similar things will happen progressively on a large scale, until there is no more resonance and connection between the human thought and the lower un-evolved levels of consciousness. Lower thought impulses will no longer have entry into our higher vibrational minds. All will be affected positively. But before we get there, we should make a conscious effort to create positive thoughts—encouraging, helping, compassionate thoughts. Is this preceding sentence necessary here? It has been used in different configurations many times throughout the book.

We are the pioneers of this work, and everyone will benefit. We will affect the whole, one particle at a time, and speed up the advancement. This method, changing our thought patterns, is the safest and most potent way to create the changes we all long for. It is difficult at first, to be sure, but battling others to make our values understood and recognized will never bring positive results. It just feeds the lower part of our personality in our emotional body. Changing our own thoughts so they reflect our own truth with peaceful strength and wisdom, without the need to force it on others, will allow our emotions to connect with our heart, and therefore, with our soul. Thus, the quality of our emotions will be transformed and will, in turn, transform the energy of people around us. No effort goes unnoticed. There is no hole or deficiency in the law of karma. Any step we take to help ourselves, rising above the natural established negative tendencies of our lower nature, will affect the whole. It will be rewarded.

In the new race, emphasis will be given to the children and the recognition of the role they play in evolution. Children will be regarded as old, wise beings, which they are, and their personalities will be nurtured as the receptacles for the higher consciousness that needs to be expressed on Earth. As we progress, a number of un-evolved souls will incarnate as well. Some will gain greatly as the energy will help them progress more rapidly and evolve quickly; others will not be able to sustain the higher vibration present in the emotional and physical planes at that time, and they will react in a negative way and will learn their life lessons through resistance. The two root races remaining to complete the cycle of the earth's evolution will speed up in their appearance and rate of evolution.

The two remaining root races are the "sixth root race," which we can already see appearing through the Indigo children, and the "seventh root race," which will complete the refinement of the human consciousness in the present round of Earth's evolution. The sixth root race will fully replace the Arian root race presently in incarnation, in less than a thousand years. During this time, the transmutation of consciousness will steadily continue. A transition is never an abrupt passing from one level to another at a fixed determined date. It takes years to infiltrate, to transform, and to reach a higher level. We are in such a transition period, and it will take about a thousand years for the transition to be completed. In terms of the earth's evolution, this is a short period of time, even if on the human scale it seems to be a long time. In our consciousness, a lifetime of seventy-two hours for a blood cell in our physical body is a very short period of time in relation to our human lifespan; and so, a thousand years seems the same on the scale of the earth.

It is as just as well that change happens gradually, as change always creates chaos. The new coming energy at first disturbs the status quo, encountering resistance from the crystallized energy already present. We are already experiencing this. It will then be followed by a more harmonious pace for all lives on Earth.

Chapter 15 -
The Stabilization of Fundamental Values

During the last two hundred years, the development of the human mind has greatly accelerated. Education is now generalized and required in the developed countries and is increasing in less developed countries. Through education, and because of our ability to receive information at the speed and depth now possible, we will see an even greater acceleration in the development of the mind.

The higher or abstract mind is the next level humanity needs to master in order to access its soul. This cannot happen without a certain amount of education and the development of our lower concrete, or thinking, mind. When the consciousness of humanity is focused in the mind, rather than in the emotions, a great step will have been taken in human achievement. It will result in greater objectivity, philosophical and psychological advancement, and, of course, progress in medicine and science. The ability to communicate around the world through the internet and other means is the embryonic stage of a greater unity among mankind. It is also an indication of the progress being made in the higher consciousness, as everything happens first on the higher levels before it reaches the physical plane.

It will help bring together races and individuals from many countries in a way that would not have been possible even twenty years ago. As the world becomes a global economy and education spreads in every country, resources will be more evenly distributed throughout the world. This will become the norm for international relations and greater fairness. At first it will be a forced partnership among nations, as the dominating countries will lose some of their power and the less developed countries will become more industrialized. What may seem to be a difficult adjustment of power in the beginning will result in a greater balance and unity for mankind.

"Equality" and "brotherhood" are not just words. They are ideals we need to implement and demonstrate in our everyday lives. Again, as everything manifests first on the higher plane before it becomes physical reality, it is encouraging to realize that this development of unity is already happening on the mental and astral planes of the earth. These levels are continuously stimulated by the more advanced beings we call the Hierarchy, or "the Masters of the Wisdom." They are working alongside advanced members of humanity from the other side of the veil. The Anteriens, being from even more evolved levels of consciousness, are also here to assist and influence the development of humanity. They are helping us because we are the most evolved consciousness in physical form upon the earth at this time, and we greatly affect the consciousness of the earth itself.

At the level of our emotional body, we are linked with the animal kingdom, influencing their behaviors and development in positive and negative ways We help in the development of the animal kingdom by involving the more advanced species, such as the dog, horse, elephant, and chimpanzee in the service of humanity. Dogs are of great help in many areas of service, such as protection, search and rescue, guidance, or most importantly as companions, giving us unconditional nurturing devotion. Horses and elephants have been used for thousands of years for locomotion, in agriculture, and in demolition and construction because of their strength. The chimpanzees are the closest to humans genetically and the sacrifice of many chimpanzees' lives, for the scientific development of treatments and medications will benefit humanity. Because all consciousness evolves through service, they are helping the entire animal kingdom evolve, and they are closing the gap between the two levels of consciousness, animal and human. Similarly, the more evolved human souls in incarnation at this time are helping the human kingdom connect to the kingdom of souls. The enlightened thoughts they create and the light they bring down are dissolving the veil of separation between personalities and souls. Both the human and animal kingdoms are helping bring their whole kingdom in closer contact with the next one above, in essence to evolve.

Humans and animals share the astral plane, so from the negative aspect, this shared astral (or emotional) level brings to animals the anger, cruelty, and fear experienced by humanity. On the positive side, when we have evolved, the animal kingdom will be transformed and their consciousness elevated as well. When peace is established on Earth, when humanity brings the love of the soul into the physical life experience, peace will touch every consciousness on Earth, including the animal kingdom and the other kingdoms in nature.

The difficulty we might experience in the course of this development is due to the divisiveness of the mind. The mind separates, categorizes, compares, and criticizes, engendering illusions such as superiority and inferiority complexes, as well as personality domination and subordination. However, as we continue to evolve, the soul energy will eventually pierce these illusions. Light will dissolve the shadow. The "will" aspect of our nature will be transformed by the love of the soul and will become the "will to good."

The more advanced of the race will allow the light to descend, first on the mental plane so those already accessing the mental level of consciousness will be beneficially affected by the light. As the number of more evolved people increases, the light will then be brought down to penetrate the emotional level, where we all connect with each other, and all humanity will be transformed. One light can enlighten thousands; all of humanity will be touched. It is important to realize that all life on Earth and beyond is like an ecosystem, only on a much broader scale. We all depend on each other. The vegetable kingdom affects the mineral kingdom through its root system and its fertilization of the ground when plants decay. In turn, the vegetable kingdom is affected by the mineral kingdom through the nutrients it finds available for its growth. The animal kingdom affects the vegetable kingdom and is affected by it, as many species depend on the vegetable kingdom for nourishment and habitat. The human kingdom affects and is affected by these three kingdoms, relying on them for survival, food, shelter, heat, and power commodities. We are interdependent with all other life forms.

As human consciousness evolves, both lines of forces—positive and negative—are activated. With iron, we build cars and machinery, yet we also build armaments to destroy each other. With the discovery of the atom we create electricity, but we also manufacture atomic bombs. We learn new ways of harvesting crops to produce more and feed humanity in larger numbers, yet for the sake of money we engineer new kinds of crops with chemicals and genetic alterations that adversely affect the health of humans and animals. This shows again why the need to elevate our consciousness to the soul is so pressing. We cannot continue to develop the mind without the wisdom of the soul.

As we enter this New Age, the choices will be made clear. We all have the opportunity to change our thoughts, if ever so slightly, and therefore change our behaviors. Remember, we create first through our thoughts. Change your thoughts and you will change your life. Open your mind to new possibilities and your life will take new dimensions, as if you opened a door that was previously closed. No one can change many things at once (unless it is through the experience of a serious trauma), but everyone can change one thing at a time, and in so doing, gradually and harmoniously evolve without the need for traumatic experiences.

Our Higher Self gives us messages and presents us with opportunities to change course and learn more useful and more prolific ways to live our lives. When we dismiss its subtle messages, our Higher Self attempts to get our attention through louder and louder messages. The challenges then presented become more and more uncomfortable, painful, and even traumatic, if need be. Therefore, it is very useful to recognize and act upon the earlier signs to avoid traumas. For this reason, it is sometimes a disservice to save our children or people we care for from their own experiences, as it will often expose them later to more difficult challenges from which we will not be able to rescue them.

It is better, for example, to allow a child in primary school who habitually forgets his books to get a bad grade as a consequence of his actions. Nobody likes to have a bad grade, so chances are he will more likely remember his books in the future. Learning this lesson in the third grade will potentially serve him better than learning the lesson later when the consequences might be more severe.

Compassion is giving a helping hand, but it does not mean we should take control and make the challenge disappear for those we love. Sometimes we try to protect our loved ones from their difficulties because of the pain and negative feelings we ourselves experience watching them struggle; our motives are not just compassionate, they are also selfish in nature. When we realize that everything happens for a reason, either for the purpose of learning a life lesson or to free ourselves from negative karma, we will welcome these challenges rather than fear them. Then we will release the pain attached to the challenges. Pain is created by resistance. Once we focus on the positive aspect of every experience in life, as there is always one, and we stop resisting, we move through our challenges with more grace and peace.

The ability to access the past and the future that we will achieve once we have connected with our soul will also give us a greater understanding of the purpose of our experiences. From the soul level, we are able to gain insights that are not available from the personality level. We will be able to recognize the karma or the lessons we are working on, and by having access to this knowledge, we will be empowered by it. This new level of consciousness and power, will, of course, bring us more responsibility, but it will also give us more freedom. Humanity will go from the stage of infancy to adulthood.

In these challenging times, our lack of openness or our willingness to participate in our own progress is directly related to the severity of Earth events. The more we resist, the more pain we will experience. When people realize that they have a say in how world events play out and they cooperate with their higher self by calming their emotions, the eventual transition will be more harmonious. This shift will happen as the number of more aware people reaches a critical mass. The Hierarchy will respond to the call of humanity and will increase the power necessary to aid in the transition. The Hierarchy cannot interfere unless we give them permission or ask for their assistance. This is the law of free will—once a greater number of people awaken and invoke assistance, help will be given. The number does not need to be half the population of Earth because the power is not measured by the numbers themselves, but exponentially, as we progress from one level to the next. Every single person counts. Every desire sent out from the heart of an individual will make a difference to the whole. Every prayer, every redirected thought toward a higher vibration will help save lives as it will minimize the anger and aggression experienced on the astral plane. Ultimately, mankind's reaction to warfare will be positively transformed, which subsequently will have a positive effect on the devic kingdom that controls and is responsible for weather patterns and Earth changes.

At this time, the vibration of the higher consciousness stepping down and infiltrating our personality disturbs the lower, less-evolved consciousness on the astral plane. The resistance these lives generate is responsible for the emotional disturbance humanity is presently feeling, as they affect us directly. We are externalizing these influences through an array of disturbing emotions that can lead us to aggression and war. For this reason, there is a great need to transfer more love and wisdom into our astral and physical levels, to produce peace and harmony. Even if this transformation takes many years to achieve, its importance has never been greater or more necessary than it will be from 2012 to 2025. The next thirteen years will afford mankind one of the greatest opportunities for healing that has ever been granted. This period is the change of the age and the balancing of our past karma.

As time passes, we will realize there is much energy with which to deal—energies that are beneficial to the advancement of the planet but are also cyclic in their effect. They will bring disruption at times, in order to replace the old established order. The presentation and sequence in which these energies will manifest will help some people progress but will also provoke negative reactions among others. Even though the energy is neutral as it presents itself, it is experienced in a positive or negative way, depending on the substance it touches. This energy will activate the negative or the positive poles of our nature according to the advancement of our emotional and mental bodies.

As we progress along the path of spiritual evolution, the un-evolved forces will be stimulated as much as the evolved consciousness. Therefore, we can expect currents of energy often going in both directions, seemingly undermining our progress. We should regard it as progress nevertheless, considering that in every situation and under any circumstance, there is always a lesson. The significance of this potential turmoil is that by the end of the period of transformation, the light will prevail, and a large number of people will have opened their hearts.

Chapter 16 -
How to Travel the Road

As we become more accepting of the idea of revolving lives, we will understand and accept more readily the essence of our life experiences. There is a need for all of us to release the old and outdated beliefs and embrace truth. The understanding of reincarnation is an important part to consider in the evolution of life. Even though not all events can be explained with the law of karma, it plays a great role in the occurrences in any cycle of growth. The law of karma is not just the law of retribution. Evolution moves forward, primarily because of positive rather than negative karma. The fact that humanity continues to progress comes from striving toward higher consciousness. Increasingly, religions will be practiced with more inspiration coming from the heart and soul rather than from superstition and fear.

The aspiration to greater love and unity inspires many; it is felt in brief moments of soul contact, produced often by devotion and idealism. Even if those moments are short-lived and spaced out, they happen—and through those experiences, progress is made. This will lead humanity to eventually access greater truth and understanding that is less and less distorted by the personality limitations.

Karma places a human being within a culture, a race, and a family that will allow for the greatest opportunity for growth in any incarnation. And if it is true that it also serves for leveling out past events, it is mainly for purifying and advancing the consciousness of the individual. Learning is one of the main goals of the soul for any incarnation, so conditions are chosen by the soul before the incarnation to further the lessons.

Another goal is the desire to push the personality toward greater altruism and pure love. The soul is inclusive of all lives. Achievement is reached when the personality becomes conscious and sensitive to all, including the ecosystem upon which it depends. The personality then regards the need for balance, the rights of all lives, and reaches the ability to coexist with all forms of life and to feel the fulfillment in this harmony. From then on, we are free from the prison of selfishness where our fears have kept us trapped for so long. In this freedom we feel gratitude, even though we have let go of some of the personality's former enjoyments. We are free of the uncontrollable drives to overindulge in food, sex, and addictions of all kinds. We have choices again. We have real control over our lives. We are free; our emotions do not have control over us any longer.

Every time someone is pulled down by negative emotions like jealousy or greed, that emotion is stimulated by fear. Fear of losing something or someone makes us prisoners. Fears hold us down. Negative emotions cut us off from our source and our birthright of happiness and joy. They keep us away from success. We become trapped in a maze of darker and lower energy forms we have created. Only light can free us from this prison and give us back the choices of thought and feeling that make us happy.

When we experience struggle in redirecting our thoughts or changing our emotions, we have the ability to call on our Higher Self and ask for it to dissolve such disturbing thoughts or emotions. "Ask and you shall receive." Our Higher Self will always respond to our call, whether we consciously recognize it or not. When we feel trapped and our personality alone cannot stop the downward spiral we find ourselves in, having recourse to our Higher Self is the most powerful tool available to us. When we ask, it will help the parts of us that feel a negative emotion and bring it back into balance. It is important that we never suppress our thoughts or emotions but dissolve them instead. To suppress emotion is like trying to put a balloon under water—it will always resurface. So pierce the balloon and dissolve the negative thoughts or emotions that have been created. The most efficient way to accomplish this is by sending a bolt of white light into it every time a negative thought surfaces in your consciousness. This will clear your energy field, and eventually you will be freed from the prison your lower emotional and mental selves have kept you locked in. With this process, your vibrations will rise and give you access to higher and greater truths without the distortion of the emotions. You will experience objectivity and loving detachment. You will live a life free of fear, with the knowledge that you are guided and protected at all times, because you will be able to receive guidance and understand the positive aspect of all events consistently.

This understanding will allow you to move through challenges without pain, as pain is only created by resistance. With understanding, all resistance and pain can be avoided. Consider that everything happens for a reason, even if you do not immediately know what it is. Synchronicity is orchestrated by our Higher Selves in order to give us opportunities. All events, as good or bad as they might appear to the personality, have a positive as well as negative side. As we focus our attention on the positive aspect of what is presented to us, we make the positive even better and the negative less prominent. We empower what we focus on. When we empower the positive, we experience more of it. When we empower the negative, we become miserable.

It is sometimes difficult to see the positive in every difficult situation, as long as we do not have conscious access to our soul. This is why we need the help of our Higher Self. This part of us is always present, always responding to our requests. Clear your energy regularly by simply asking your Higher Self to dissolve pain, anger, fear, or any other negative feelings you may be experiencing, and to do it safely and harmoniously. This will clear the way for more light to come down and stop your entrapment in the spiral of darker and denser energy. This clearing is necessary in order to receive Higher Self guidance, because we are cut off from our Source-conscious connection as long as we are trapped in our lower emotional body.

Judgment and criticism foster separation and hatred. Competitiveness and greed foster aggression and entrapment. Jealousy is only a sign of insecurity. All these feelings are generated by fear and keep us separated from empowerment. Our mind has the ability to create. We need to be aware where are we directing our mind so that it can create for us. What are we choosing to focus on? What are our intentions? Do we want to get even, get revenge, be right, control someone else? . . . or do we want to be free and feel empowered? There are choices to be made in every moment of our life: choice of actions to be taken, choice of which thought to empower, choice of which word to speak. Do we choose harmlessness? Do we choose kindness? Are we letting our emotions entrap us in pain and misery? These are choices that we need to be conscious of every moment of every day of our lives, until through our constant awareness and determination we set ourselves free from our lower emotions and thoughts. These repeated choices will eventually bring our mind to connect with higher planes where fear becomes void. They will no longer be part of our reality. These choices will not be our burden any longer, as we will have dissolved our negative thoughts over time. Our mind will eventually be re-patterned with new ways of thinking. It will now be connected to the vibration of our soul. The personality will no longer be trapped in lower consciousness; we will be free, guided along the path of our soul.

This time of transformation represents the ending of an age, and yet we cannot talk about the end of an age without talking about the coming of a new age. Fear of the disruption created by the transition period dominates our collective imagination. Thus we lose sight of the bigger picture: that all this effort is ultimately for the greater good of all and that important evolutionary gains await humanity in the coming new age. It is necessary for everyone to reflect more on the coming of this new age, as it will help us to manifest it faster and in a more powerful way. Contemplation on the end results of the transformation will also help us "see the light at the end of a tunnel." As we stay focused on the benefit of the transformation, we will move through it with much more strength and hope, diminishing the intensity of the turmoil in the universal consciousness. This will create a much easier transition for everyone.

The power of thought is capable of channeling a potent projection of energy and needs to be understood and regarded as a tool for creation. Fear attracts what we fear. Love attracts love, and it's not just the thought that creates; the intensity of emotion accompanying the thought will greatly impact the experience we will live through individually and as groups or nations. Your heart will never guide you to hate or kill, but your lower emotions might. Watch any desire that arises from fear; it will only add to the destructiveness and your entrapment in darkness. Evaluate your thoughts and desires from the perspective of your heart. No matter how dark the personality may be when the soul speaks, there is only compassion and understanding.

You will not transform darkness by opposing it; you will only transform it through understanding and love. Darkness will be transformed by enlightened thoughts and desires. Darkness is only transformed when it comes in contact with the light, not when it is met with more darkness, such as intolerance and judgment. Whoever your God may be, pray to him for love, and you will discover his essence. You will only communicate with the beings of darkness if you pray for revenge or pray with intolerant righteousness. The latter only leads to complete entrapment by the darkness of the un-evolved mind and will pull you further away from the light. Resentment and revenge projected on anyone keeps you enslaved to them. You attach yourself to them through these dark emotions. Only light can break such ties and set you free. Furthermore, when your energy is vibrating with the high vibration of love and light, the projection of darkness from others will be dissolved upon impact and will no longer affect you.

The same intensity of emotion, when projected toward the light, allows us to rise and connect to soul, producing the feeling of bliss that comes with such heightened experience. This connection, unfortunately is rarely constant; but because of temporary experiences with soul contact, people can mistakenly believe they are being guided by God, even when they are no longer in this state of connection. Their lower mind takes over and the guidance they receive is simply the reflection of their own thoughts and convictions. In special moments of soul consciousness, insights may come, but once those who have had such experiences are reclaimed by their personality in the everyday life, the less-evolved form of their nature takes over, pulling them away from the beauty of this divine connection. It is important to differentiate these states of consciousness, so that we can access genuine soul guidance, rather than the animal instinct of the lower self. This is evolution, and it will lead us to a true expression of God's will and consciousness on Earth.

The presence of un-evolved lower forms of consciousness on the physical plane is generating a lot of turmoil at this time. This energy is surfacing to be transmuted and purified as part of humanity's evolution. There is no purification without transformation of energy, and this transformation of energy necessarily creates turmoil. Infusions of light are affecting the darkness, generating reaction and resistance, and amplifying its resonance. Consequently, the activation of darkness generates reactions and surges of emotions among people, such as aggression, cruelty, selfishness, or fear.

The activation of light, however, amplifies its resonance through the desire for peace, love, and unity. None of humanity is perfected at this time. Most people feel both polarities in themselves. The lower form of their nature is activated along with their more advanced consciousness. This results in the use of anger and rage to defend peace, or force and aggression to see their values prevail. Higher values cannot be defended with the methods generated in the lower un-evolved forms of our nature. When these lower forms of emotion surface in our personalities, we should transform and heal them, not express them as raw emotions, no matter how valuable the originating cause is in our eyes. Humanity is called to evolve into the level of the mind. Our thinking ability is what differentiates us from the animal kingdom. To continue using our raw emotions as the driving force for our actions is keeping us trapped in our animal nature. To use our mind to help our emotions calm down is a mark of our higher human capabilities and our level of development. As long as humanity uses its ability to think and reason to follow its lower nature or emotional urges, darkness prevails and is even strengthened. As long as we cannot emerge from the lower mind and incorporate light into our energy field, we will encounter chaos. This chaos is the consequence of the conflict between the two forces of light and darkness, or soul and lower personality. The infusion of light into all levels of our personality and in our life is necessary to generate progress and evolution.

During the Atlantean times, destruction occurred because the dark forces on Earth were prevailing. The principle problem has not changed. The one we call God will not allow us to destroy his body, as this would impede the law of progress or evolution. If we do not raise our consciousness, destruction will happen again.

So no matter what the circumstances, do not let emotions stir up anger, hatred, or fear. When these negative emotions do surface, ask your Higher Self to help the parts of you that feel those emotions and that generate those thoughts. Say quietly, "Higher Self, dissolve that thought." Do not let negative thoughts take over; purify them, so that you can realign to the light without delay. Forces will eventually help stabilize and balance all consciousness upon the earth. Remember, it is not about killing or destroying darkness but about transforming it. Lower forms of energy are life, in the same way that light is a living consciousness. Life cannot be destroyed, but it can be transformed. When darkness is absorbed by light, it becomes light. So the battle is not a fight, it is a healing. We all should remember that every human being emanates from the same source and will return to the same source. No one will be rejected or excluded. Once evolution has brought the last one of us back to the Source through healing and the transformation of the lower nature, the earth itself will evolve, and a cycle will be completed. We all originate from and belong to the same source, so we should provide a shoulder of support for each other to achieve this progression together, rather than push each other down. Helping others helps ourselves and ultimately helps God, of whom we are all a part.

So what can you do today to help someone evolve? From an act of kindness to an enlightened thought shared, every one of us can do something simple that will help the light and the love to anchor on Earth. This descent of higher vibration will help the lower forms of energy evolve, just as the alchemy of the earth transforms and purifies metal into gold, or rocks into precious stones.

The alignment of planets in and beyond our solar system plays an important role in the distribution of energy in and around the earth. We are part of a greater whole and a greater consciousness. Energy is in constant movement. How we respond to these cosmic energies dictates our rate of evolution and our life experience. Even though we have no control over the infusions of energy, we have control over how we let them affect us. This choice is the prerogative of humanity, once we choose to control our emotions and rise to the level of mind. We can transform these energies through our thoughts and choose how we want them to affect our personalities. If we don't, we let them stir up our emotions and create chaos in our lives. The use of our mind to raise our consciousness and employ energies in their positive aspect will enhance our progression and advancement. Let us exercise choice consciously and rally our Higher Self to help us implement the proper choices. We cannot do it from our personality's lower levels alone, but we can do it with the assistance of our Higher Selves.

Chapter 17 -
The End of Distress

Beyond the year 2025, all of us will make great progress in rebuilding society based on greater unity and balanced human relations. The rewards of this transformation will be so immense that it will usher in much hope, and with it, a new vision of the future. We do not need to wait until then to make necessary changes and progress toward this future. A lot of old beliefs can be released, such as the belief that people or the world cannot change. Everything can be changed, and everything will. Nature is in constant evolution, and so are we. That which is crystallized and cannot adapt to the new energy will die. It will come back in a new form, a new body, for a fresh start to continue its evolution. This is true for individual forms in any kingdom in nature, but it is also true for organizations, institutions, and ideologies. All that which is created in the mental or emotional level is as alive as that created on the physical plane. Thoughts influence our daily living as much as our environment and physical limitations do. They generate emotions and desires that influence our daily decisions.

Thoughts are the basis of all creation. Our beliefs create the framework from which our personalities evolve. Our personalities are composed of beliefs inherited from our family of origin and those which come from our past life experiences. We are also subjected to the thoughts governing the country we live in, the religion we adhere to, the race we have chosen to incarnate in, and finally, the universal consciousness of the human kingdom. Thought forms that originated in larger group consciousness influence us as well. We call them "group karma."

But within these influences, we have choices. Every one of these choices will affect our personalities and will affect the whole. We can let ourselves be burdened and accept the status quo of the lower mind, or we can be driven to think outside the box and expand beyond our limitations. We have examples of this from our great philosophers through the ages, and leaders throughout history, who have forged new realities and expanded our thinking. Those great men and women were not the only ones capable of doing this; we are doing it too, each one at our own level.

The transition we are going through, which will be emphasized and implemented in 2025, is here to help us move our thought projection beyond present limitations. We can create new paradigms in all the levels of consciousness within our association. We are going to do it en mass because of the injection of light sent to us by higher levels of consciousness entering our energy fields. This higher vibration of energy will and already is challenging us to evolve faster in these special times of our current development. We can resist and create chaos, or we can embrace the light and move through this evolving period with harmony.

Everyone will do what they are capable of from where they stand. If we make a clear decision to be flexible and embrace these changes, we will be given assistance by our Higher Selves to move through this transition with ease. We will receive guidance in the form of thoughts that our Higher Self communicates to us, allowing us to understand the positive outcomes of situations we each find ourselves in, if we are open to it. This understanding will help us accept changes with more ease. Guidance may also come through new opportunities presented to us. Sacrifices are not painful when we are making them of our own accord, knowing that the value of what we will gain from them will greatly surpass what we have let go of in their wake. Our intent and reactions will determine the outcome; change your thoughts and you will change your life.

The more dramatic the changes, the more outstanding the results will be. What can you change in your life today that would help you shift, if ever so slightly, your alignment with the Universe? What is the thought that you can redirect that will change the nature of your mental and emotional bodies? What is the spiritual practice or visualization you can incorporate in your daily life that will help you change the energy you are projecting around you? What is the negative thought or emotion that you can consciously dissolve every time it surfaces in your consciousness until it is not there anymore? You know what they are. They are the ones that make you unhappy, uneasy, depressed, angry, frustrated, or uncomfortable. The thoughts that generate those emotions are telling you that you are not creating in harmony with who you really are. Pay attention to those low vibration thoughts and choose to dissolve them. With time they will all disappear, and you will not even remember that you once harbored them.

That is how you change—one thought at a time, making deliberate choices. You might believe at times that you are entitled to your anger or your resentment because someone caused you pain or distress. In those moments, remember that these feelings are hurting you more than they hurt the person they are directed toward. Love yourself enough to choose to rise above the feelings, so you can be happy instead of being tied down in the lower levels of consciousness by the self-imposed anchors of negative thinking and the damaging emotions they generate. Whatever you project will manifest. Any energy you put into motion will come back to you, unless you make a conscious effort to dissolve it immediately.

We have put a lot of energy in motion during this Dark Age, which we are now leaving. We can dissolve many dark thought-forms with the light we bring. We can redirect this energy, freeing it from old encumbrances and use it for more positive creations.

Life can be good and enjoyable. It is largely a matter of perception. When you count your blessings, you feel fortunate and blissful. When you only see what you do not have or what you have lost, you are depressed and miserable. Joy cannot be magnetized by projecting misery. You need to change the focus of your thoughts in order to change your feelings, and therefore, change your vibrations, consequently changing what you magnetize.

The work of transformation starts there. Find anything in your life that brings you a good or happy feeling. Energize those feelings. Focus on them. Dwell on the thoughts that give rise to those feelings, as this will open the door for more of those kind of feelings to enter your life. Choose happiness over being right. If something is taken away from you, it is either because karmically you do not deserve to have it, or you have something to learn from the loss. If it was unduly taken from you, the Universe will replace it. It will give you back what you lost and better. Trust this! In every case, it is a gain for you, not a loss—either you free yourself from a karma, or you experience more lessons and gain in learning. Choose to see it that way and you will progress with great speed. This positive perspective will inhibit all feelings of anger, frustration, revenge, betrayal, or pain. It will keep you in the higher vibration of gratitude. Darkness will not have power over you any longer, and your life will be the reflection of the inner peace you have found.

The present time is a reflection of the past, but it is here to be transformed, not to be repeated. Even though we are influenced by the past, we need to learn from it and move forward. The experiences and the knowledge acquired should be used to strengthen and enrich us, not impair us. Healing is the ability to choose to move forward in new experiences, activated by a loving heart and guided by the wisdom acquired from past events. The ability to gain from experiences rather than being impaired by them is the quality and mark of advancement. It represents the point of contact with the higher mind, the higher consciousness that allows us to see beyond the initial reaction of the lower selves, the personality.

As we progress in our development, the influence of the higher mind's expanded understanding allows our personality to free itself from the confines of the prison of limited thinking. As our mind perceives other realities and integrates them into its thought process, it enlarges its capacities and frees itself from its limited and selective perception of righteousness and false beliefs. This is the first step toward cultivating wisdom and liberation from constrictive thought forms. We can achieve this progression by making deliberate choices and through the use of various healing methods, or progress will be imposed on us by world events, and will bring about uncomfortable situations.

Our present time represents such a period of expansion for humanity. When one's heart is opened, changes become easier because they are accepted and understood. There is no resistance. When the personality's perception is overshadowed by fear of survival in its different aspects, whether fear for one's life or fear for one's comfort, disruptive events are always more painful because they are misunderstood and resisted.

This is a time of great evolution, and everyone will gain from the elevation of consciousness and the unity that will result. The various levels of our soul's evolution, expressing themselves through physical personalities, require different avenues for expression. People cannot focus on opening and cultivating their minds if they do not have the bare necessities for physical survival. Yet everyone can still evolve through acts of kindness and the demonstration of love toward one another. The realization that they are not alone in their pain or their fear allows the heart to open in gratitude, even if only periodically, and soul connection can be experienced during these moments. For the more advanced souls or more fortunate personalities, education stimulates the mind and eventually pushes the personality to search beyond the generally accepted knowledge. This yearning to know and understand more brings growth and expansion.

Desires are the propellers of growth at all levels of consciousness. At first, emerging desires are oriented toward personality satisfaction and personal pleasures, but as one matures they are followed and enhanced by soul stimulation. When the soul is very young, the process of soul stimulation takes many lifetimes. The personality evolves without the soul influence or guidance, lifetime after lifetime, until some level of altruism is reached.

Society plays a great role in our experiences. Acceptance or rejection, support or pain—we are molded at first by our surroundings. Only when we evolve in our consciousness can we say we have choices. Being able to weigh what we want or what we feel deep inside against what we have been taught allows us to eventually rise above the illusion of limited knowledge and slowly expands our consciousness. This process can be greatly enhanced by the most advanced souls presently in physical incarnation who are here to teach in various departments of societal affairs. They have been called at this particular time to help in the descent of knowledge and light, stimulating the mind of humanity. These people, "the New Group of World Servers," are here in these challenging times to help in the elevation of consciousness. A great "soul advancement" will result for them and for the ones they touch through their work.

Everyone, of course, is encouraged to participate on the level of their own ability, as no matter where we are on the ladder of evolution, there is always someone we can help. The descent of light and of goodwill is essential for the progression of humanity and the dissolution of the negative karma created during the Dark Age. It is the tool that will allow for and foster harmony during this transition period and minimize chaos.

There are no special methods that must be followed in order to actively participate in this work, even though tools such as mantras, meditation, or visualization are very helpful and encouraged. The expression of compassion in any form is really the only thing required. The practice of compassion includes acceptance, harmlessness, the giving of assistance to the ones among us who cannot help themselves, and the demonstration of love and gratitude in one's daily life.

The future is not cast in stone. The future is created and transformed by humanity as we progress. Whatever has been written and predicted throughout the ages by different cultures around the world regarding 2012 does not really matter. If this transition period is inevitable, the way we move through it is not ineluctable. It is up to us now, as we are in incarnation at this time, to mold and to transform all the events through our thoughts and our way of being, influencing all lives and all consciousness. Miracles start with us. If we can procreate by giving birth, we can co-create at a higher level and bring a better reality for the ones we bring to life. We have more power than we think. We need to recognize it, claim it, and use it with positive intent. This is what we are called to do in this new age. Let the transition be seen for what it really is: a bridge to a better world.

Inherited circumstances cannot be avoided, but we can choose to regard them either as handicaps or opportunities. If we resist and blame them for our unhappiness and our difficulties, we are empowering their negative aspects, and, of course, we will experience more pain as we resist them. If we look at them as opportunities to learn and better ourselves, we move through them with graciousness and greatly gain in our evolution. Pain is the precursor of joy if we choose to learn from pain, but it becomes our burden when we unknowingly choose to interpret painful events from the personality perspective as dreadful and unfair.

The lack of recollection from one life to the next has great benefits, allowing us to start anew without the burden of the regret, love, or hatred of the past. It also has its handicaps, as it prevents us from understanding experiences in our life that result from karma created in previous lifetimes. However, the further humanity evolves, the closer we come to accessing our subconscious minds and retrieving the information collected over the ages and stored in what is called "the akashic records." At this more advanced stage of our development, we will be able to use the information available in the akashic records to better ourselves rather than retaliate or suffer from the recollection. This is due to the fact that in our progressive reach toward this higher consciousness, we will have developed wisdom along with a greater sense of love and compassion. We receive more knowledge as we gain the ability to access it and to apply it, as we progress in our maturity, following the same pattern of learning that takes place from childhood to adulthood.

Furthermore, the progress made from one generation to another in education speeds up the development of the mind and affects the whole of human consciousness. This progress allows the clearing of the illusions created over the ages and opens us to greater truth.

One might wonder how long it will take for humanity to evolve, considering the billions of people on Earth who are still deeply embedded in their emotional bodies. The incarnation of more and more evolved souls will transform the universal consciousness in a significant way, pulling all of humanity to higher levels.

Once we have passed this difficult transition from one age to another, symbolized by the year 2012, we will progress in a more rapid and powerful way. The years between 2012 and 2024 will be a healing period and will lead to the transformation of consciousness, which the Fourth Ray—the Ray of Harmony through Conflict—will bring about, starting in 2025. The people in incarnation at the time will be challenged to open to the path of real spirituality, the path of brotherhood and compassion. The events we are experiencing in our present challenging times will have opened us to this energy, and many will rise to the level of soul consciousness. Great progress will follow, and some have predicted that this time will be followed by a thousand years of peace. Needless to say, even if this number is symbolic, great progress will be made during this New Age. It will be called the Golden Age.

One of the first effects of this progression is that the energy of money will be rendered positive, and therefore it will be attracted by people projecting a higher, more positive energy. This means that money will be used by more advanced people for the benefit of all humanity in an enlightened way, rather than for war and individual power.

The elite will be wise men and women, and governments will be composed of a council of those more advanced souls, rather than the perverted and manipulative individuals we often find at the head of governments of countries or organizations today. The commercial exchanges will be structured under a world council, which will take into consideration the needs of every country for a fair exchange of their resources. It is easy to understand that once fairness is the rule and the guide for our actions at all levels of power, peace will be a normal consequence. Of course it is still a distant reality, but we can fathom it, knowing that the energies entering into the consciousness of the earth, which we call the Rays, are coming to help us in this evolution. The sequencing of the Rays is purposely scheduled by divine intent to push us in this evolution.

When the time comes for you to participate on a greater level of involvement, according to your own sphere of awareness, you will be presented with opportunities to do so. You will be called to choose, as always, to take those opportunities . . . or not. If you are afraid that you will not recognize these opportunities, ask your Higher Self to make you aware of them as they are presented to you, and you will recognize them. If you miss one or choose not to participate at a given time, other opportunities will come later. However, it is important for us to realize that if we are in incarnation at this particular time, it is because as a soul, we have chosen to be here and therefore to participate in this transformation and will gain from it. So if you choose to ignore these opportunities, you are not following your soul's path or intent.

Resisting the soul's direction is always difficult, because when we do, we are going against the flow of our soul's path. When we are in the proper alignment with the energy flow of our soul, all becomes easy, and our needs as physical beings are met. We just need to have faith in the process.

But it is exactly this faith that many of us lack—and that the coming of the New Age will help us develop. Behind all the drama and all the fear, the light is doing its work, and evolution is inevitably marching ahead. After the wrath of the storm comes the sun. Light will always prevail, and it is our role on Earth to help it manifest more quickly. Remember, the choice is yours.

Bibliography

Bailey A.A. *A treatise on White magic.* New York: Lucis Publishing Company, 1934

    Esoteric Healing, New York: Lucis Publishing Company, 1953

    Letters on occult meditation, New York: Lucis Publishing Company, 1922

    Esoteric Astrology, New York: Lucis Publishing Company, 1951

    Telepathy and the Etheric vehicle, New York: Lucis Publishing Company, 1950

    Esoteric Psychology—Volume 1, New York: Lucis Publishing Company, 1936

    The Externalization of the Hierarchy, New York: Lucis Publishing Company, 1957

    The Seventh Ray: Revealer of the New Age. New York: Lucis Publishing Company, 1995

    A treatise on Cosmic Fire. New York: Lucis Publishing Company, 1925

    Letters on Occult Meditation. New York: Lucis Publishing Company, 1922

Langley, Noel and Hugh Cayce. *Edgar Cayce On Reincarnation.* New York: Warner Books, 1967

About the Author

Josiane d'Hoop is a metaphysical leader who has helped thousands of people through her various healing methods. As the founder of the nonprofit organization Quantum Institute International, d'Hoop teaches and spreads the knowledge of the ageless wisdom worldwide, and how it is applied to the everyday human endeavor.

Born and raised in Paris-France, she currently lives in North Carolina with her family.

Websites: www.walkthruthedoor.com
www.qiionline.org

www.ingramcontent.com/pod-product-compliance
Lightning Source LLC
Chambersburg PA
CBHW031324290526
45784CB00014B/976